WHAT WE REALLY KNOW

ABOUT

SHAKESPEARE.

BY

MRS. CAROLINE HEALEY DALL,

AUTHOR OF "HISTORICAL PICTURES RETOUCHED;" "THE COLLEGE,
MARKET, AND COURT;" "EGYPT, A PRESENTATION;"
"LETTERS HOME FROM COLORADO, UTAH, AND
CALIFORNIA," ETC.

87116

"Alle that he doth write
Is pure his owne."
LEONARD DIGGES, 1640.

*PR 2894
.D14 W*

SECOND EDITION.

BOSTON:
ROBERTS BROTHERS.
1886.

ST. JOSEPH'S UNIVERSITY
PR 2894 .D14W   STX
What we really know about Shakespeare.

3 9353 00027 1971

Copyright, 1885,
BY ROBERTS BROTHERS.

𝔘𝔫𝔦𝔳𝔢𝔯𝔰𝔦𝔱𝔶 𝔓𝔯𝔢𝔰𝔰:
JOHN WILSON AND SON, CAMBRIDGE.

PREFACE.

———◆———

A FEW years since a gentleman of some scholarly
reputation was asked to deliver an address, on
Shakespeare's birthday, before a Shakespeare club
of which I had long been a member. He spoke
before two or three hundred people. He represented Shakespeare as "vilely born," — the son of a
butcher, apprenticed to a butcher, without education, a pot-house brawler, loafing about with poach-
ers, until he got himself into such serious discredit
that, after an enforced early marriage, he was obliged
to fly from his native town. He then proceeded to
glorify that Divine Spark of Genius, given to its
possessor without regard to his deserts, which had
set this pot-house brawler above all mortal men.
What was my amazement to find that among his
audience no one beside myself was prepared to
question any of these statements.

As the public discussion of the Baconian origin of Shakespeare's Plays has proceeded, the principal argument of its supporters has been found in our ignorance of Shakespeare's life, and in the assumption that most of the above statements are true. Whoever proves them to be mainly unfounded will therefore help to form a rational public opinion.

During the last winter I listened to three different addresses from the author of " Atlantis," who thinks he has discovered a cipher in the First Folio, and that the story concealed by this cipher claims the Plays of Shakespeare as the work of Lord Bacon !

Mr. Donnelly had a large audience, and on one of these occasions he addressed a literary club, and was answered at some length by two or three fair Shakespeare scholars. He stated in substance that Shakespeare was low-born, vilely bred, led an obscure life, and was a man who might easily be hired to cloak the personality of a superior who feared political disgrace.

Many of Mr. Donnelly's statements have been long ago as effectually refuted as the story of Shakespeare's relationship to Sir William Davenant; but I observed that when his opponents rose, no one of them was prepared to controvert his statements with hard facts, but each spoke in an indefinite and weakly way, chiefly about his own opinions.

To bring forward these facts became my duty on the 23d of April, 1885, when I was asked to address the Shakespeare Club in the city of Washington. I care very little for adult people who are ignorant of what is now well known to every student of Shakespeare. It is true that of the books put forth by Mr. Halliwell-Phillipps, Dr. Ingleby, and Mr. French, only small editions were printed, and the volumes are very expensive; but in this country, at least, the many public libraries furnish all sincere students with the opportunities needed.

It was to the young and untaught that I spoke. What I said was received with much enthusiasm, and I was asked by several of the best-read men whether I could not put it into a handbook which every child could buy.

This I am now trying to do.

1. Shakespeare's origin is said to have been obscure. He is sneered at as the son of a butcher.

I expect to show that his family took root in the yeomanry of England, and that on both sides it looked back upon a reputable history.

2. It is stated that his education was deficient, that he was taken early from school, and apprenticed to a butcher!

I expect to show, by the testimony of those who knew him, that his education was considered deficient only in a technical sense; also that his removal from school on account of his father's poverty is a deduction from circumstances which have been exaggerated; also that there is no proof that he was ever apprenticed to anybody; while it is much more likely to be true "that he understood Latin pretty well, for he had been in his younger dayes a schoolmaster in the countrie,"— a statement made by Aubrey in a manuscript of 1680, and never before quoted as having significance, so far as I know.

3. It is stated that his character was low and his companions of the baser sort.

I expect to show that for the age in which he lived, his character was remarkable for steadiness, moderation, and thrift, and that his intimates, so far as known to us, were of the best sort.

4. It has been stated that he was little known to his contemporaries.

I expect to show that he was widely known and much beloved. In a time when there was no newspaper and no magazine, when the modern "interviewer" had never been heard of, Dr. Ingleby finds one hundred and eighty-five references to Shakespeare on record within the century, and fifty-seven of these were made during his lifetime. If we omit the testimony of the newspapers and magazines, if we remember how few people of his period could read and write, would Tennyson or Longfellow make a better showing?

5. The uncleanness of Stratford is brought forward in this discussion, as if to sustain the statement that Shakespeare was of low birth. Without pausing to argue the matter, I would suggest, that, in the reign of Elizabeth, London was as filthy as Stratford. The fresh rushes strewn daily over the floors of her Majesty's palace covered the worst abominations of the kennel and the pig-sty. If Southampton had ever gone down to New Place, he would have found nothing to astonish him. Among the early settlers of Massachusetts Bay, there were many men sprung, like Shakespeare, from the ranks of British yeomanry, and others of higher estate still, who crossed the ocean in search of fresh air and "faire water," where it might be possible to rear their infant children. These emigrants came not from Stratford but from Essex, Lincoln, Northumberland, and Devon.

As my outline of the Life of Shakespeare pretends to small originality, I have not paused to use quotation marks even when I use the very words of better authorities. My own individual speculations I hope I have made sufficiently clear. I did not consider it necessary to incorporate into the Life the appearance in print of every Play. Those who desire to follow the public career of the poet will find ample material in the noble volumes of Halliwell-Phillipps. My first object was to give to the Life a mortal body; to show what sort of man the poet was as he walked through the world.

In the Appendix I have desired as far as possible to condense and abbreviate whatever I have quoted. I frequently reduce a page to a few lines, or a few lines to a phrase, but I have had no deliberate intention of altering words or their spelling. I have done this at times involuntarily, to simplify the understanding of them for young readers.

The scholar who for this cause complains of my method, will not be the student for whom these pages are written.

CAROLINE H. DALL.

1667 THIRTY-FIRST STREET, WASHINGTON, D. C.
May, 1885.

CONTENTS.

———◆———

AUTHORITIES.

Charles Knight's Life of Shakespeare.

Preface to Theobald's Shakespeare, 1767.

"Shakespeareana Genealogica," G. R. French, London.

"The Centurie of Prayse," C. M. Ingleby, London, 1874.

Spedding's Letter to Judge Holmes.

"Outlines of the Life of Shakespeare," by J. O. Halliwell-Phillipps. Five Editions, from 1872 to 1885 inclusive.

WHAT WE REALLY KNOW ABOUT SHAKESPEARE.

WHAT WE REALLY KNOW ABOUT SHAKESPEARE.

———•———

AN OUTLINE OF THE LIFE OF WILLIAM SHAKESPEARE.

WILLIAM SHAKESPEARE, the poet, was the child of Mary Arden and John Shakespeare, both of families belonging at that time to the great class of agricultural property holders called "yeomanry," although both seemed to have retained traditions of a higher condition.

It was claimed by some authorities, as well as by John Shakespeare himself, that at the battle of Bosworth, Aug. 22, 1485, an ancestor of his received a "coat of armour" for "faithful and approved service" to Henry VII., and was rewarded with "lands and tenements." In 1550, sixty-five years after this took place, Richard Shakespeare was living at Snitterfield as the tenant of Robert Arden. This was three miles from Stratford, and there lived with him his two sons, Henry and John. Henry rented a large farm near Snitterfield church, and seems to have been until his death steady and well-to-do, — content with his country life. John was undoubtedly of other metal, — ambitious, adventurous, and anxious from the very first to build up a family and accumulate real estate.

On the other side, Robert Arden's father was groom of the chambers to Henry VII. French says that he was a favourite and received grants of land. Robert was therefore well endowed. In the application for a " coat of armour " he is called "Esquire." He had seven daughters, and of these Mary, the mother of William Shakespeare, was the youngest; yet for some reason she occupied the most prominent position under his will, dated Nov. 24, 1556, just a year before her marriage. A certain sum of money was given her, and all Wilmecote, and the estate called Asbyes, consisting of fifty-six acres and a house, and the crops in the ground. Her sister Alice was a widow, and is provided for by a life residence in her father's house and certain properties. Mary had also a house at Snitterfield near Richard Shakespeare, who was, as we have seen, her father's tenant. It was perhaps in matters connected with the management of this farm that she first grew intimate with

John Shakespeare. Her father left a small gratuity to every householder in the parish of Aston "not able to *own a team*," which indicates a man of some position. The inventory of his goods, and later the inventory of those of his second wife, attest the same fact. Tapestries, or "peynted clothes," a chafing dish, brooches, eight oxen, two bullocks, seven kine, four horses, and three colts, in addition to a flock of sheep, indicate luxuries as well as comforts.

In October, 1556, John Shakespeare purchased two small freeholds in Stratford, which shows that he was himself prosperous, and in fit position to marry an heiress like Mary Arden. The marriage took place some time in 1557; for Joan, the oldest child, was born Sept. 15, 1558.

There were fifteen hundred "houselyng people" in Stratford in the thirty-seventh year of Henry VIII. That John Shakespeare was industrious and respected is shown by his rapid rise in office.

In 1557, before his marriage, he was made ale-taster;

In 1558, a burgess;

In 1559, a constable;

In 1560, an affeeror, or magistrate to impose arbitrary sentences;

In 1561, a chamberlain ;

In 1562, again a chamberlain ;

In 1565, an alderman ;

In 1568, the high bayliff or mayor, — an officer who held courts in all causes involving amounts of less than thirty pounds.

It will be seen that he passed steadily through all the offices in the gift of the town, and a single circumstance seems to indicate that he was of superior rank to most of the men so serving. Nowhere, in connection with his nomination or appointment to these offices, is his vocation designated. He is styled " Shakespeare," " Mr. John Shakespeare," or " John Shakespeare, yeoman." Thus in September, 1567, Robert Perrot, brewer, Mr. John Shakespeare, and Ralph Cawdrey, butcher, were nominated for high bayliff. If John Shakespeare had been only a butcher or a glover he would have been called so ; but here he is " Mr. John Shakespeare," and in the legal papers of the period he was either " John Shakespeare, Gentleman," or " John Shakespeare, yeoman." A *yeoman* is defined by Blackstone as " he who hath free land of 40 shillings per annum, and who was antiently thereby qualified to serve on juries, vote for the knight of the shire, and do any other act whereby the law requires one that is ' probus et legalis homo.' "

When elected alderman in 1565, Shakespeare was the only one of the bench to whom no calling is attributed.

Mr. Halliwell-Phillipps calls him a glover, on the strength of a legal process executed before his marriage, the title being given as follows by Mr. French in his "Shakespeareana Genealogica," p. 387 : " An action was heard before John Burbage, June 17, 1556, against John Shakespeare : Thomas Sache de Arschotte in comte Wigorn versus Johannem Shakspeare de Stretford in comte Warwicki, glover in placito quod reddat in octo libras," etc. Mr. French asserts that this is the only instance in which the term is applied to John Shakespeare ; but Mr. Halliwell-Phillipps alludes to an entry in the Corporation books and a recognizance in the Controlment Roll of the twenty-ninth year of Elizabeth, making three entries in all, covering a period of thirty years.

John Shakespeare was however primarily, like all his kindred, an agriculturist, raising sheep, oxen, and horses on his rural properties. Cattle were killed, skins were dressed, and wool was baled upon his estate, and one of his Stratford houses was used as a depot for his products. From 1557 to 1575 his fortunes seem to have prospered. In 1564, when the plague visited Stratford, the

Shakespeare family was almost the only one which escaped the touch of death. Mr. Shakespeare contributed to the relief of the poor and plague-stricken in that year, after the fashion of a man of substance. His wife had already lost two infant girls, probably from the want of proper sanitary conditions in the town. She may have learned, from that experience, how to protect herself by cleanliness or flight. Her exemption is the more remarkable because it was in this year that William Shakespeare was born. He was born in Henley Street, where John Shakespeare seems to have owned two contiguous tenements. The late researches of Mr. Halliwell-Phillipps have shown that one of these was used by him as a residence, and the other, at least on its lower storey, as a shop for the sale of wool. The most western was the house in which Shakespeare was born; and the room to which this tradition has always clung is the only suitable chamber, with a large open fireplace, in the tenement. At some very early period, perhaps to accommodate the poet's nine brothers and sisters, doors of interior communication were opened in the upper storeys between the wool-shop and the house.

In 1848 this whole birthplace estate was bought by subscription, and became the property of the

Corporation. This was largely, if not entirely, due to the well-sustained efforts of Mr. Halliwell-Phillipps.

In March, 1565, John Shakespeare and one of his colleagues made up the accounts of the borough for the previous year, a work often performed with counters and "entered" by professed scriveners. He probably showed a capacity for the work, for he was employed again the next year, and a sum equivalent to thirty pounds of present money was paid him by the Corporation.

In two respects at least this father resembled his famous son. He was a good business manager, and he was fond of the drama. It was when he was mayor that the Queen's players first came to Stratford. In those days, when the players entered a town they offered an opening entertainment free to the people in honor of the chief magistrate, and they then received from him whatever gratuity he thought fit. In this way, payment was made by "Mr. Shakespeare to the 'Queen's players,'" and the "Earl of Worcester's players." This taste for the drama had doubtless been stimulated by the "Mysteries" performed at Coventry, and by the strolling companies of the neighborhood. At all events, it was strong enough to be inherited, for not only did his son William go upon the stage, but a younger son Edmund; and one of the sons of his daughter Joan, William Hart, became an actor.

Mr. Halliwell-Phillipps says that both Shakespeare's parents were wholly illiterate; and he doubtless bases this conclusion upon the "mark" attached to the signatures of both. I think the probabilities are the other way. It is quite possible that John Shakespeare was able to make up the town accounts without the aid of a scrivener, for many persons used a mark at that time as a *rapid* way of making a legal signature. Few persons wrote with ease; the general style of writing required slow and patient endeavour, and the same person sometimes used two or three kinds of marks. In this opinion I am sustained by Lord Campbell, and also by many facts in the early history of New England.

In speaking of the poet, Rowe wrote in 1709: " His family were of good figure and fashion then, and they are mentioned as gentlemen."

In October, 1566, Gilbert Shakespeare was born. He is said by Mr. Halliwell-Phillipps to have gone into business in London for a time, but if so, he relinquished this when his brother became a landowner, for he was for many years his business manager at Stratford. In April, 1569, Joan Shakespeare was born, the poet's only sister, for whom he showed such tender consideration in his will. A sister Anna and a brother Richard followed, but Richard left no descendants, and Anna died in infancy. The time of Gilbert's death is not positively known; but it probably occurred on Feb. 3, 1612. At all events, he must have died before Shakespeare, as he is not mentioned in his will.

Before his marriage, John Shakespeare owned two freeholds in Stratford, one of them the Henley-Street house; and in 1570 he held fourteen acres of meadow land under the Cloptons, and perhaps a residence on or near this land may explain his removal from the board of corporators in the town. In 1575 he purchased two houses in Stratford. I cannot help thinking that, in his ambition to found a family and accumulate real estate, his troubles may have begun. Three years later he mortgaged his wife's farm of Asbyes to Edmund Lambert, who had married her sister Joan, for £40, — money which was perhaps made necessary by the purchase in 1575. Five years later it is seen that Edmund Lambert refused to receive payment to lift the mortgage at the time agreed upon, because Shakespeare owed him other money, which he could not then repay. The son, John Lambert, urged a settlement after his father's death;

and in 1597, all compromises refused, John Shakespeare filed a bill for the recovery of Asbyes.

The story of the bailiff's decline in fortune is
not very clear; he is said to have been in prison
for debt when he filed this bill. But there was
another John Shakespeare in Stratford, a shoe-
maker, who was always in trouble, and perhaps
the affairs of the two have been somewhat mixed.
Beside this, the registry of the courts has been
lost from 1569 to 1585. It seems to me that very
mistaken inferences have been drawn from the
fact that in 1578 John Shakespeare was taxed
on one half his property in Stratford, and after-
ward not at all. In 1579 he is styled a yeoman;
he may very likely have been living outside the
town limits on leased property, and no taxes
within the borough may have been due. It is not
common for municipalities to consider the poverty
of tax-payers, and I think it was never known
that taxes were remitted for that cause. John
Shakespeare's position was a hard one. He had
sold the Arden property at Snitterfield to redeem
Asbyes, with no better result than a lawsuit; but
he was not ruined. He did not forfeit his Stratford property, for his son received it from him un-
impaired; and it was in the year before he filed
his bill for its recovery that he applied for a grant

of "armour," — an application that would have
been absurd in a man of falling fortunes, or a
debtor in prison.

In 1599 a second application for a "coat of
armour" was made, and French says that it was
granted. A coat meant something in those days,
and would not have been granted on false pre-
tences. If it had been so granted, the jealousy of
his son's contemporaries would have been prompt
to proclaim the theft, nor would Shakespeare's
children have dared to mount it above his monument in such a case.

French says: "At all events, the plain, un-
equivocal language of the best heralds is, that
John Shakespeare was entitled to impale, and his
descendants to quarter, the ancient arms of Arden
of Wilmecote, a gentleman of worship and an
esquire, with a motto that declares, —

> 'Non sanz droict,' —
> 'Not without right.'" [1]

Whatever comfort coats of arms might give was
reserved for the next generation, however.

In 1592 John Shakespeare had been found ap-
praising the goods of Henry Field, who was the
father of the London printer, who brought out his
son's "Venus and Adonis" the next year.

[1] See pp. 110–116.

In 1596 his brother Henry died, and on the
8th of September, 1601, John Shakespeare was
buried. He appears to have retained his faculties
to the last, as he was concerned in an action
brought by Sir Edward Greville against the town
in the same year. His widow survived him until
the 9th of September, 1608. It would be pleasant to know something more of her, for it is not
unlikely that the poet inherited from her some of
his finest traits; and he survived her but a very
short time. Her influence, whatever it was, must
have been felt through his whole life.

We have followed the life of John Shakespeare
to its close. We have seen that it was that of a
man prominent in the eyes of his towns-people.
Now that we understand his history, we shall be
the better prepared to understand the life of his
oldest son.

William Shakespeare was baptized on the 26th
of April, 1564. Judging by the customs of the
time, he was probably born on the 23d; and that
day is now celebrated as his birthday. Stratford
was by no means a bad locality for the education
of a boy such as Shakespeare must have been. It
was on a great highway. All sorts of merchandise were brought to its fairs, and all sorts of people came with the merchandise. The fairs and

theatrical performances at Warwick, Kenilworth, Coventry, and Evesham were not too far away for the wandering and adventurous feet of a bright boy. Nothing could be more romantic and lovely than the scenery surrounding his native town; and he probably travelled on foot from one farm to another, spending his holidays and Sundays on the farms of his kinsfolk and acquaintance, as well as in the diversions at the fairs. His plays are full of allusions which show an intimate acquaintance with the habits of flowers and insects, and are entirely free from the superstitious notions and errors of his time. Such superstitions he sometimes quotes, so that we know he was not ignorant of them; but he was a lover of nature, and as careful an observer as Bewick.

The country teemed also with historical traditions. The great epochs of English history had left impressions at once poetical and stirring on all the neighboring soil, — had involved all the families he knew. Stories of "Bosworth field" his grandfather must have heard at first hand in his youth, and had doubtless often repeated to the growing boy. His plays bear evidence that he was also familiar with the "Mysteries" at Coventry.

About the year 1570 Shakespeare probably entered the free school, and before that he must have

been taught to read and write; for this was the
condition of entrance. In the year 1578 his
father's circumstances began to suffer. When he
borrowed money of Roger Sadler, however, a friend
was found to stand security, and within a year after
he mortgaged Asbyes he was ready to lift the mortgage. By the loss of the records of the courts for
sixteen years, covering this period, we are deprived
of what might have been valuable information.
Mr. Halliwell-Phillipps takes the traditional view
that Shakespeare was removed from school on
account of his father's poverty; but so far as I
have been able to ascertain there is not a particle
of proof of this, nor of the story that goes with it
that he was apprenticed to a butcher. A school
like that at Stratford would certainly have been
soon exhausted by such a boy; and that his first
employment would be found among the yeomen
who were kindred to his father and mother is
altogether likely. A great deal has been said
about Shakespeare's deficient education; but he
had more education than many eminent men in
America. One of the most widely read men I
ever knew, in many languages, had only one six
weeks of schooling in his lifetime, and bought
a copy of Ovid's "Metamorphoses" when he was
sixteen, with sixty cents which he had first to

earn by picking hickory-nuts. The stories of the learned blacksmith and of Robert Collyer are familiar to this generation. As the question is, however, of great interest, it seems better to introduce here certain statements in regard to it than to reserve them for the Appendix.

Ben Jonson had said of his friend that he had "small Latine and lesse Greeke."

In 1680 Aubrey, commenting on this, says: "Yet he must have understood Latin pretty well, for he had been in his younger years a schoolmaster in the countrie;" and quotes a Mr. Beeston as his authority, — a statement in accordance with my feeling that he would soon be done with the Stratford schools; for if he ever taught at all, it must have been between his fourteenth and his twentieth year.

In 1638 Jasper Mayne writes:—

"Who, without Latine helps hadst been as rare
As Beaumont, Fletcher, or as Shakspere were?"

In the same year Ramsay wrote of Ben Jonson:

"That Latine Hee reduced and could command
That which your Shakspere scarce could understand."

In 1691 Gerard Langbaine says in "England's Dramatic Poets:" —

"I am apt to believe that his skill in the French and Italian tongues exceeded his knowledge in the Roman languages. I esteeme his Playes beyond any that have been published in our language."

In 1606, during Shakespeare's lifetime, a "Criticism on English Poets" appeared, in which Burbage and Kempe, two prominent actors, are represented as giving instruction to university students; and that Ben Jonson's criticisms were not always considered apposite may be seen from the following passage : —

"Few of the University," says Kempe, "write Plaies well; they smell too much of that writer Ovide. Why here's our fellow Shakspere puts them all downe, I and Ben Jonson too. O that Ben Jonson is a pestilent fellow! He brought up Horace giving the Poets a pill, but our fellow Shakspere hath given him a purge," etc.

It is probable that many of Shakespeare's friends resented the words of his critic. In 1658 Richard Browne expressed a common feeling when he wrote :

"Ben Jonson said to Shakspere, 'I will draw envie on thy name,' and then threw in his face 'small Latine and lesse Greeke' !"

In 1662 Thomas Fuller says, in his "Worthies of Warwickshire :" —

"William Shakspere was born at Stratford upon

Avon; in whom three eminent poets may seem in some sort to be compounded, — Martial, Ovid, and Plautus. Many were the wit combats between him and Ben Jonson. Jonson was built far higher in learning, solid but slowe, like a Spanish galleon; Shakspere, like the English man-of-war, lesser in bulke, could turn with all tides, tacke about, and take advantage of all winds by his quick wit and invention."

Rowe, writing in 1709, says : —

"Ben was proud and insolent, so that he could but look with an evil eye on any one that seemed to stand in competition with him." And further he adds : "One play of Shakspere's was founded on the 'Menæchmi' of Plautus; that is, his 'Comedy of Errours,' and of that I know of no translation so old as his time."

How great Shakespeare's technical knowledge of Latin might have been, we shall probably never know; but his *feeling* for other languages no appreciative reader will be likely to mistake. He never uses a foreign word when an English one will answer. There is no affectation in his use of ancient or modern tongues, but he was too sincere an artist to turn the "*Et tu, Brute*" of the dying Cæsar into English. He felt the poetic force of the Latin phrase.

In his Preface to Shakespeare's Plays, Theobald
says, in 1733, that the current opinion of Shakespeare's learning has been determined by Jonson's
squib. He leaves his readers to judge from passages in which Shakespeare imitates the classics,
whether this is to be trusted. "How happily he
could imitate them," he says, "if that point be allowed, or how gloriously he could think like them,
without owing anything to imitation! . . . 'T is
certain there is a surprising effusion of Latin wordes
made English (in his works), far more than in any
English author I have seen, but we must be cau-
tious how we imagine this was of his own doing.
For the English tongue in his age began extremely
to suffer by an inundation of the Latin."

The truth of this concluding remark is proved
in the writings of both Bacon and Milton, the
latter certainly not anxious to recommend himself
to Elizabeth or James.

It must certainly have been to the Stratford
school that Shakespeare owed whatever knowledge of English, Greek, and Latin he possessed.
Another way must be found to account for his
knowledge of the continental languages, remarked
by Langbaine, and the intimacy with the French
testament, commented upon by Singer, in the Chis-
wick edition of his Plays. Shakespeare had not

the contempt for the English tongue which Bacon
manifested, and often used the words of a translation, as in the case of North's translation of Plu-
tarch, where a very small knowledge of the Greek
would have carried him to the original had he
cared in the least about it.   His enjoyment of the
humours of school-keeping was frequently shown in
later life ; and as far as we can judge, as teacher or
scholar, he was familiar with the "Accidence," the
" Sententiæ Pueriles," Lilly's " Grammar," and the
few classical works which were in those days
chained to the desks of a free school, as the Bible
was chained to the church pulpit.

According to all authorities, Shakespeare had
hardly been free of the Stratford schoolhouse four
years when he married Anne Hathaway.   He was
not nineteen till nearly six months after, and we
do not know exactly when he was married.   Probably a pre-contract, the equivalent of a legal marriage, had been entered into in the summer of 1582,
for his first child, Susannah, was baptized May
26, 1583.   In a private note Mr. Halliwell-Phillipps
informs me that there were no registers of pre-
contracts, and a notice of one would only be found
by an accident, as in litigation papers.   No such
paper exists in this case.   At the same period,
before a license could be taken out for the ecclesi-

astical ceremony, — the pre-contract being considered as a civil rite, — it was necessary to lodge at the Consistorial Court, a bond entered into by two sureties, certifying that there was no impediment of any kind to the marriage. Such a bond has been found in this case, dated Nov. 28, 1582, and the sureties were two neighbours of Richard Hathaway of Shottery. Perhaps it was from that fact, and also because this bond had attached to it the seal of some Richard Hathaway, or rather a seal bearing the letters R. H., that Anne Hathaway has usually been considered the daughter of Richard Hathaway of Shottery. I think, however, that could hardly have been so. Richard had died the previous year ; and his will, which does not mention any daughter Anne, was proven July 9, 1582. Anne may have been a ward or niece, and the seal attached to the bond must have been borrowed only. In the bond itself she is called Anne Hathaway of *Stratford*, not Shottery. The will of Richard Hathaway is of Richard Hathaway of Shottery.

Shakespeare's marriage has always been the subject of many coarse and unsympathetic jests, which seem to be wholly unfounded. If he had been guilty of any scandal, we must have heard of it, for he was in a position very soon to rouse all the

enmity and ill-will of his fellows. He was handsome, successful, and, without college breeding,
easily gave college-bred men "a purge," as a contemporary tells us. In addition to this, he soon
grew very rich, and had great influence with his
own towns-people. In London he was well known
to fellows who had grown up in Warwickshire.
When he went back to his home, he went to
the near relatives of those who, as actors or publishers, were conversant with his London life. Had
there been any scandal connected with his story,
or had he lived unhappily with his wife, the
spirit which pointed the "small Latine and lesse
Greeke" would certainly have chronicled the fact.

Before he was twenty-one, he was the father of
three children; yet not so well taught by experience, that he did not get into some serious trouble
with a certain Sir Thomas Lucy, of Cherlecot near
Stratford. The loss of the records of the courts
already alluded to, is as vexatious to the scholar, as
the loss of the medical diary kept by Shakespeare's
son-in-law, Dr. Hall; for if we had those records,
we should know whether Sir Thomas actually
prosecuted Shakespeare and for what.

Whether he really was led into stealing deer
two or three times, as Rowe relates, or whether he
only took the part of the deer-stealers in a sting-

ing lampoon, we shall never know. At all events,
he had made Warwickshire too hot to hold him,
and about 1585 departed penniless and alone to
London. He may not have been very sorry to go,
for he must have felt the need of a broader life
long before this; but his journey was undoubtedly
a hard one. His father could have given him no
assistance at that time. Having reached London,
he would naturally have sought out Warwick men,
and it was probably at the suggestion of one of
these that he tried to make himself useful about
the theatres. The story of "Shakespeare's boys"
has always seemed to me a very pleasant one.

If Shakespeare was introduced by any Warwick
man to Burbage, who was the proprietor of the
theatre, he found it in the parish of Shoreditch, far
away in the fields; and Burbage, who kept horses
for his customers, may have suggested his first step.
There were few private coaches, and none to be
hired in those days. Men rode on horseback to
the play, which was performed in the afternoon,
and their horses were held by boys picked up at
the moment. Shakespeare was so well suited to
this trust, that he soon saw an opportunity to or-
ganize a small band of helpers, who were so well
liked, that before alighting, every gentleman, it was
said, soon learned to call out for "Shakespeare's

boys." The story carries its own evidence even if
it had not been told by his god-son. Who does
not recognize in it the thrifty, capable man who
bought New Place, the finest house in his native
town, in twelve years after the day in which he
fled from it penniless ?

Between 1587, when he took some part in the
proceedings between his father and uncle in regard to Asbyes, and 1592, five whole years, we
know absolutely nothing of Shakespeare, yet these
years must have been full of work. Books could
be had for the first time, and men of culture
showed him their fine points. Where he was, and
what he did, during this period may never be
known. My own conviction is that he spent it,
after some apprenticeship at the theatres, chiefly
on the Continent. This conviction is founded on
the internal evidence of the Plays, and has nothing
to support it beside, save vague traditions. At
the time of the "Tercentenary," there was a three-
days' festival at Frankfort; and at the same time
a novel was published founded on a tradition that
Shakespeare had visited Frankfort, and that one
of his comedies had been written there and performed before the Court.

Some years ago a photograph from a picture of
Hamlet was sent me, which is still hanging in my

library. The original is in the Royal Gallery at
Copenhagen. That was painted in the twelfth
century, and the tradition in Copenhagen is, that
Shakespeare had seen it. If the story be not true
it ought to be, for we do not detect the outer man
of Shakespeare's hero, in its "inky cloak" and
"nighted garments," more certainly than we be-
hold his inner likeness in the eye filled with spec-
ulation, and the mouth, the wavering sweetness
of which indicates a man incapable of steadfast
resolution. Long ago Harriet Martineau drew
attention to the fact, that Shakespeare showed a
familiar acquaintance with the household habits
of the Italians, which she supposed impossible, in
his time, to one who had never been in Italy.

In speaking to Lord Ronald Gower, Taine said
that Shakespeare had made a special study of the
works of the early Flemish engravers, and that he
had made use of some of their works and their
allegorical figures. The French critic asserts that
the line in Hamlet, "Like Niobe, all tears," occurs
beneath one of these engravings, in which the
"mobled queen" appears as in a masque covered
with tear-drops. A visit to Italy, on Shakespeare's
part, would explain the actual or pretended paint-
ing of his portrait by Zucchero, which seems to be
disproved if the poet never left England.

Robert Greene, in his outburst of jealousy, in 1592, calls Shakespeare an "upstart crowe," which he would hardly have done if the poet had been steadily rising in his profession in London for the last seven years. The insult to the poet was resented by "divers of worship," persons of wealth and standing, who could easily have made acquaintance with him on the Continent. None of the public mentions of Shakespeare occur before 1594, which would be incredible if he had actually been resident in London since 1582. If any discovery in relation to Shakespeare's life upon the Continent should ever be made, it must be made upon the Continent, and not in England. The attention of continental scholars to the points in discussion should therefore be urged.

In a recent number of "La Domenica Litteraria," a prominent Roman journal, Signor A. R. Levi draws attention to a minute knowledge of Italian literature on Shakespeare's part. There is a well-known passage in Othello, —

> "There's magic in the web of it,
> A sibyl . . .
> In her *prophetic fury* sewed the work."

In the 46th canto and 80th stanza of the "Orlando Furioso" is the following : —

> "Una donzella de la terra d'Ilia
>   Ch' avea il *furor profetico* congiunto
>   Con studio di gran tempo e con vigilia
>   Lo fece di sua man di tutto punto," —

which we may translate, if we are average Italian
scholars, as follows: "A damsel of the land of
Ilion, who united *prophetic fire* to long and careful
study, set every stitch with her own hand." The
root of the word *furore*, which is usually translated "heat," was just the sort of word to strike
the poet's fancy, and when his genius had changed
the word *fire* to *fury*, it made him owner of the
phrase. At that time there was no translation of
the "Orlando," except one published by Sir John
Harington. In that translation this whole stanza
was omitted.[1]

Signor Levi finds the familiar exclamation of
Iago, — "Who steals my purse steals trash," —
and so on, paralleled in a stanza of Berni's "Orlando Innamorato," which had never yet been
translated.

Let us remember, in this connection, that in
1691 Gerard Langbaine wrote that Shakespeare's
knowledge of the French and Italian tongues exceeded his knowledge of the Roman, — that is,
the Latin. Yet a moderate school-knowledge of

[1] See Boston "Daily Advertiser," July, 1885.

the Latin was a more common accomplishment in his day. How was it possible for him to be familiar with French and Italian if he never left England?

It has never been exactly understood how Dr. John Hall, who married Susannah Shakespeare, came to Stratford; but if Shakespeare were, as I think, a travelled man, he might easily have fallen in with Hall upon the Continent, and have induced him to settle there.

A very interesting book, by Cohn, called "Shakspeare in Germany in the 16th and 17th Centuries," was published in London in 1865. It relates rather to the progress of Shakespeare's drama in Germany than to his own possible appearance there; but it contains several interesting suggestions.

It was in 1585 that the Earl of Leicester went to the Netherlands, at the head of the troops Elizabeth sent to the aid of the United Provinces. Sir Philip Sidney, writing from Utrecht, speaks of "Will, the Lord of Leicester's jesting player." It has been imagined that this player was Shakespeare.[1] Bruce thinks it was rather Will Kempe; and unless an *alibi* can be proved, it might have been Richard Tarlton, the famous comedian, who

[1] See John Bruce, in papers of the Shakspere Society, vol. i. p. 94.

was almost certainly the "pleasant Willy" of Spenser. Tarlton died in 1588, and complimentary verses indicate that he was known by that pseudonym.

Dr. Bell, in the "Morgenblatt" (4to, Stuttgardt, 1853, No. 50), assumes that Shakespeare went to Germany by way of Holland, where he might have made acquaintance with his "Niobe, all tears."

It is interesting to know that Leicester, while in the Low Countries in 1591, commended an English company of players to the king of Denmark. These players went abroad to improve themselves by travel, and played to provide for their expenses.

An imperial notary, named Ayer, at the Court of Nuremberg, wrote plays from 1593 to 1605, and it seems clear that Ayer and Shakespeare must either have had a personal acquaintance, or have derived materials for their work from some common and, so far, unrecognized source.

As early as 1611 Shakespeare's "Merchant of Venice" was acted at Halle. Can we suppose him ignorant of this fact? In 1626 four of his Plays were performed at Dresden by English comedians. But it will be said, how did it happen that, if Shakespeare went to the Continent, there is no allusion to such a fact in the papers which relate to him? How did it happen that, when Abraham Sturley wrote to Richard Queeney in London, urging him to talk with Shakespeare about Shottery yard-lots and Stratford tithes, Queeney was never forced to reply, "Our Will is away in foreign partes"? We know that Shakespeare was obliged often to travel into the provinces with his company, although the absence of his name from the provincial records lends strength to the idea that he may have gone abroad. No record remains of these provincial journeys. If any exist of his presence abroad, it must be found upon the Continent. Of the proof in the Plays themselves, this is not the place to speak. No insular breeding shows itself upon his pages.

If any scholar could be found competent and willing to devote himself to a search for traces of Shakespeare in France, Germany, the Low Countries, and Italy, as Mr. Halliwell-Phillipps has devoted himself in England, it is possible the problem might be solved.

At all events, the five years from 1587 to 1592 were fruitful of growth. On the 3d of March, 1592, Shakespeare's first play, the first part of "Henry the Sixth," was brought out by Henslowe. The scene of this play, it will be observed, is laid partly in France. Its great success must have been as much a surprise to Stratford and London as it would have been if his friends in those two towns had been as ignorant as we are of his whereabouts meanwhile; and one of the first proofs of this was found in a posthumous tract by Robert Greene, a distinguished dramatist of that time, called "The Groatsworth of Wit." By this time all Shakespeare's plays of the reign of Henry VI. were probably on the stage, and Greene travesties in his pamphlet a vigorous line in the third Part thus: —

"There is an upstart crowe, beautified with our feathers, that with his '*Tiger's heart wrapt in a player's hide*' supposes he is as well able to bumbast out a blanke verse as the rest of you, and being an absolute *Johannes-factotum* is in his own conceit the only Shake-scene in a countrie."

Greene died on the 3d of September, 1592, and his book was published by Henry Chettle soon after. This passage created so much disturbance that Chettle was obliged to apologize for printing it. It is a valuable passage, for it shows us that before he became an author Shakespeare had made himself useful in all sorts of ways as a theatrical factotum. We see also that he had already made powerful friends; for in his apology, after speaking of Shakespeare's courtesy and excellence as an

actor, Chettle goes on to say, " *Divers of worship*
have reported his uprightness of dealing " and his
" felicitous grace in writing."

There was in London in those days a certain
Richard Field. He was from Stratford, and made
himself remarkable in 1589 by printing a superb
edition of Ovid's " Metamorphoses." In 1593 he
brought out the " Venus and Adonis " of his young
townsman, which was for a long time as popular
as if its daintiest graces had been readily per-
ceived; but whatever may be thought of that,
" Lucrece," published in the May of 1594, immediately secured to Shakespeare the position of one
of England's *greater* poets. The prefaces and dedi-
cations to these poems are the only papers remaining to us of Shakespeare's writing " which may
be supposed to have individual character," says
Mr. Halliwell-Phillipps. For myself I think his
whole treatment of the story of " Venus and
Adonis " most individual and worthy of profound
study. Sensuous as its pictures are, they are
painted by a chaste spirit. That he had the leisure
to write these two long and remarkable poems
was probably due to the prevalence of the plague,
which put a stop to all theatrical performances for
more than a year.

As one of the Lord Chamberlain's servants,

Shakespeare acted before Queen Elizabeth at Greenwich, and there he was associated with Kempe and Burbage.

At Christmas, in 1594, the "Comedy of Errours" was played at Gray's Inn. This elegant hall, finished in 1560, is one of the only two structures known to us which may have echoed to Shakespeare's voice. In 1596 Shakespeare was living in Southwark. By this time he had probably outlived his trouble with Sir Thomas Lucy, and went from Stratford to London once or twice a year. His "Romeo and Juliet" now took the town by storm, and his earnings were so large, and his father's position so much improved, that the latter was ready to apply again for a "coat of armour," and Shakespeare to purchase New Place in the following year. But before this could happen he must have gone back to Stratford to attend the funeral of that only son for whom he had pleased himself by accumulating honours. A little later he lost his uncle Henry at Snitterfield. Certainly if Shakespeare's early life had been marked with disgraceful scandals or excesses he would at this time have removed his wife and family from Stratford, and founded a new home in the neighbourhood of London. He was able to do as he chose, and he chose to go back to those who had always known him, who showed confidence in his character and means, and where he might continue in frequent intercourse with his own kindred.

In 1598 the quantity of corn which he raised shows him as one of the most successful agriculturalists of the town.

It made little difference to Shakespeare practically whether his family were in London or Stratford, so long as he led the life of a player. That was a wandering life spent in travelling from province to province. He had some residence in London, for he was assessed in Bishop's Gate in 1598, and it was in this year that he did Ben Jonson the service of securing the acceptance of " Every Man in His Humour."

We can guess that the respect which was shown him in Stratford he had also earned at the theatre. He was not only a good actor and a great poet, but he was a generous and kindly man, of good critical judgment, or he could not have saved this play, which the managers wished to refuse. He laid out a fruit orchard at New Place, and a few years after he planted the famous mulberry-tree so long associated with his name. Mulberries had been brought to England by a Frenchman named Vertin, and their distribution was sanctioned by King

James.   On the fifteenth of January, 1598, when he was negotiating the purchase of thirty acres of land in Shottery, Abraham Sturley wrote to Thomas Queeney, in London, suggesting that as Shakespeare had money to spare it might be well to induce him to bid for the town tithes.

In a private note Mr. Halliwell-Phillipps tells me that "just before the Reformation the clergy got frightened in regard to the security of their properties in the future, and in many cases accepted bonuses for long leases.   In this way the tithes at Stratford had been 'leased,'" and it was now proposed that Shakespeare should buy the remaining term of one half these tithes.

In this letter Sturley alludes to Sir Thomas Lucy; and in the opening scene of the play of "The Merrie Wives of Windsor" the author so unnecessarily revives Lucy's memory that it would seem as if he had in some way brought himself afresh to the poet's mind, — a matter, as will be seen elsewhere, closely connected with the history of the "coat of armour." [1]   Queen Elizabeth had been so fascinated with the humour of Falstaff when he called himself Sir John Oldcastle, that after the name was changed by her order, to save the feelings of the Oldcastle family, she ordered

[1] See pp. 110–116.

Shakespeare to show her Falstaff in love, and the "Merrie Wives of Windsor" was produced, probably in 1598.

In Sturley's letter we see Shakespeare regarded as a man of wealth. The writer wants Shakespeare to purchase the tithes because it would benefit the Corporation. He desires Queeney to tell Shakespeare that it will benefit *him* and make him useful "frendes." He was evidently in the secret of Shakespeare's ambition. A little later Queeney himself writes to "his loving good friend and countryman," Mr. William Shakespeare, asking for a loan of £30, and he is not refused.

Shakespeare's increase in wealth is often pronounced incredible; but at least two other actors of his time accumulated large fortunes. So little, however, could Shakespeare's Stratford friends understand the rapid rise of his fortunes, that they asserted that it was the bounty of the Earl of Southampton that enabled him to purchase New Place.

This suggestion is interesting because it shows us how intimate his relations with Southampton were supposed to be. A man is judged by his friends, and the associates who chose Shakespeare or were chosen by him bear witness to a refined taste. Ben Jonson and Marlowe were men of so much literary ability that the alliance was natural. It is sometimes said that we are not to judge Shakespeare by his works. That was not the opinion of Jonson, who wrote of the Plays:—

> "Looke how the father's face
> Lives in his issue."

It seems to me, that in the liberal political views obvious throughout the Plays, we have the secret of Shakespeare's attraction for many persons of superior rank. In his lifetime he was doubtless the mouthpiece of the liberal party; and that nothing worse happened to him than some order to omit the deposition scene in "King Richard II.," was due to his prudence and his personal charms. The picture which Jonson draws of him is captivating. Pembroke, Rutland, and Montgomery, as well as Southampton, were his friends, and when the "Corporation" want favours at Court they rely upon the poet's influence.

The Earl of Pembroke was said to have been the "most esteemed and beloved of any man of that age." There are many proofs that Shakespeare continued on excellent terms with all those with whom he was most associated. Of his especial Stratford friend, Julius Shawe, the records of the Stratford Corporation speak in the highest terms.

This social influence was added to his power as a dramatist, and so, by 1598, the booksellers began to be anxious to get his Plays.   Certain "sugared sonnets," written apparently for his dearest friends but carefully hidden from the public, began to be talked about.   These Sonnets, certainly the finest of the period, contain many passages well known to all modern readers.   It seems to me that they are ideal, yet that here and there they throw light, by impulsive words, upon the history and character of the author.   It has been said that Shakespeare never knew the value of his own verse.   Why then did he write in the 55th Sonnet, —

> "Not marble, nor the gilded monuments of princes,
> Shall outlive this powerful rhyme"?

That Shakespeare himself loved and valued the drama, I fully believe ; but he was a young man when he died, and he had retired voluntarily from the stage long before.   When therefore he wrote in the 111th Sonnet, —

> "And almost thence my nature is subdued
> To what it works in, like the dyer's hand," —

I believe he was expressing his annoyed consciousness of the estimate others put upon his vocation.

The same feeling was expressed by some lines

4

written to him by John Davies in 1610, in the
" Scourge of Follie:" —

> " Some say, good Will, which I in sport do sing,
>   Hadst thou not played some kingly parts in sport,
>   Thou hadst been a companion for a king
>   And been a king among the meaner sort."

The first publisher who attempted to publish the
Sonnets, however, only succeeded in getting hold
of two ; but the poet's reputation led to the issue of
forged pieces, of false titlepages, and advertisements
that the publisher was "about to issue a new play
which had never been on the stage." Shakespeare
seems to have had too much to do to pursue these
frauds, or else was supremely indifferent to them.
His apathy led a certain Thomas Pavior, residing
at the suggestive sign of the "Cat and Parrots,"
to bring out a play under his name with which he
had certainly nothing to do ; that of "Sir John
Oldcastle."

It was in this year, also, that the first edition
of "The Passionate Pilgrim" appeared. This was
a fraudulent collection of small poems, published
with the name of Shakespeare upon the titlepage.
It was printed by one

" W. Jaggard,

at London, St. Paul's Churchyard,

in 1599."

Of twenty poems, only five were actually written by Shakespeare. In the third edition of 1612 appeared two of Heywood's, who complained bitterly of the abuse, while he acknowledged that Shakespeare was in no way responsible for it. One belonged to Barnfield, another to Marlowe, and others still were the property of unknown authors. Shakespeare's name was finally removed from the titlepage, probably in consequence of his own remonstrance. That it ever appeared there is a striking proof of its commercial value. This publication has a definite interest for the student of Shakespeare; for here appeared for the first time some of the "sugared sonnets" of which Meres had written. They are the 138th and 144th of the edition published in 1609; and their appearance in this piratical fashion seems to show that they were stolen from private albums, and lends colour to the idea that all the Sonnets were separately written, and were never intended as a series.

In this year, 1599, the Globe Theatre, which the genius of Shakespeare was to make the most famous in the world, was built; and Southampton went "merrilie to the plays every day." In March of this year the ill-fated Earl of Essex started for Ireland. Southampton went with him as his General of Horse. Both he and the Earl of Rutland had married into the family of Essex, and Shakespeare's affections must have been largely interested in their fortunes. While it was still supposed that Essex would return victorious from Ireland, the poet inserted a graceful compliment to him in the play of "King Henry V." Many fraudulent attempts were made to print this play. In the same year, according to French's Genealogy, John Shakespeare received his grant of "coat armour." His grandchildren certainly used it, and it was placed above the poet's monument, — proceedings which, taken in connection with the motto, would have been likely to start many satirical pens, if not founded upon a well-established claim.[1]

About the same time Shakespeare brought an action against one John Clayton for £7, and recovered it; and at this time he tried very unsuccessfully to mix philosophy with poetry in a contribution to a volume called "Love's Martyr," by Robert Chester.

In February of 1601 the Earl of Essex was beheaded, and while Shakespeare's heart was still sore with the imprisonment of friends and the political situation, his father died, and was buried September 8. The absence of court records leaves us unable to account for the fact that John Shake-

[1] See pp. 110–116.

speare made no will.   If his embarrassments were as
great, in 1580, as Mr. Halliwell-Phillipps supposes,
the poet might have purchased his estates and dis-
charged his obligations; but it seems clear that he
did not do so.   He had but two brothers at home,
Richard and Gilbert, and Gilbert was certainly
in his own employ.   Edmund was with him in
London; and Joan Harte, his only sister, partly
perhaps because her own circumstances were nar-
row, and partly because her mother needed her
care, was apparently living in Henley Street with
her children.

In the following January the appearance of the
exquisite drama of "Twelfth Night" at the theatre
and at Court was followed by the purchase of one
hundred and seven acres of land in Stratford from
William Combe and his brother; and as the poet
was in London, conveyance was made to his
brother Gilbert, who seems to have acted from this
time as his agent.

In the following September Walter Getly sold
him a cottage and garden in Chapel Lane.

"Hamlet" was the next drama which challenged
public interest, and as usual, several fraudulent attempts were made to print it.

On the 2d of February, 1603, Shakespeare was
summoned to Whitehall to play before the Queen.

On the 24th of March she was dead. Many were the voices lifted in mourning. Scarce a poet of any degree kept silence; but Shakespeare did not speak. Three several times was he reproached publicly with his silence, — by the author of "Epigrams," by the author of the "Mournful Dittie," and by Henry Chettle. In no way did he respond. The woman who put Essex to death and imprisoned Southampton need expect no more favour from him than the friend who had betrayed him.

In 1603 King James granted a license to nine players, of whom Shakespeare was one. It is noticeable that he speaks of them as already "king's servants," from which it has been supposed that they may have played before him at Perth in 1601. It is said the company were introduced in Scotland — at Aberdeen — by a letter from the King. The "king's servants" took rank with the grooms of the chamber, and had a "dress" allowance.

In the same year Shakespeare purchased of one Underhill a "messuage, with barnes, gardens, and orchards."

Fraudulent publications went on; and according to Heywood, in one instance at least, Shakespeare was sufficiently annoyed to interfere.

In the same year he prosecuted Philip Rogers for a debt that he owed him, and received a bequest of thirty shillings in gold from Augustine Phillips.

In July, 1605, the poet made what Halliwell-Phillipps calls the most judicious purchase of his life. He gave £440 for the unexpired term of a half-interest in a lease, extending to 1636, of the tithes of Stratford, Old Stratford, Bishopton, and Welcombe, subject to certain annual payments. Seven years before, this purchase had been pressed upon him, as a reliable citizen certain to serve the interests of the town. Only a man of great prudence and tact could make such a purchase profitable to himself, as the tithes were frequently paid in produce, in sheaves of wheat, and pigs from the sty, which must be again disposed of.

In October of the same year Shakespeare's company performed before the mayor at Oxford; and he stayed, in all probability, with his friends the Davenants at the Crown Inn. In the following spring Mrs. Davenant brought her husband a son named William, who was baptized on the 3d of March, 1606, at St. Martin's. The boy was Shakespeare's godson, and very fond of him; but the fact gave occasion to the only scandal which has survived concerning the poet, and for-

tunately it has met with complete refutation, as
may be seen in the contemporary documents col-
lected and published by Halliwell-Phillipps. Sir
William Davenant's father was a morose but excellent man, who had a beautiful, lively, and
witty wife.   For the pleasure of both, Shakespeare stayed with them as he went back and
forth from Stratford to London.   It was a suspicious circumstance that the story of the scandal
had been printed, with other names attached
to it, in a volume of "tavern-jests," in 1630.
It was first put in shape by that old gossip Aubrey,
who acknowledges that it was not known in Shakespeare's lifetime, as he was held in great esteem at
Oxford!   It is repeated after Aubrey by Gildon in
1699; by Hearne, 1709; "The Poetical Register,"
1719; in the conversations of Pope; and the manuscript of Oldys. The scandal that "was not known
in Shakspere's lifetime" is now effectually put
to rest, — first, by John Davenant's will, in which
he not only mentions his "son" William, but
makes generous provision for him; and speaks of
his wife as a mother who would have guided his
children safely, had she not died a fortnight before
him.   The second refutation is to be found in
certain poems, which could have been nothing
but wanton insult to the memory of the dead, had

there ever been any doubt of Mrs. Davenant's
virtue. Here are the concluding lines of one of
them : —

> "What merits he ? Why, a contented life,
>   A happy issue of a virtuous wife,
> The choice of friends, a quiet, honoured grave, —
>   All these he had ; what more could Davenant have ?"

Langbaine and Wood, of Oxford, in giving the
history of William Davenant, both distinctly assert
that he was the "mercurial son of a saturnine
father, Mr. John Davenant."

In 1636 Sir William Davenant wrote of Shakespeare : —

> "Beware, delighted Poets, when you sing
> To welcome nature in the early Spring,
> Your numerous feet not tread
> The banks of Avon, — for each floure
> Hangs there the pensive head."

It does not appear that Shakespeare was a great
actor, but certainly he shows himself in "Hamlet"
the very finest of dramatic critics. Sir William
Davenant asserted that he had seen Taylor act
"Hamlet," who, having been taught by Shakespeare,
taught Betterton how to act it. If Shakespeare
taught any one, — and it is very probable that he
did, — it must have been Burbage, as Taylor did
not take the part till after Shakespeare's death.

In 1606 "King Lear" was played before King
James. Late in November of 1607 the booksellers and the company obtained the consent of
the Master of the Revels to the publication of the
tragedy, two editions of which appeared in 1608.
The author's name is given in large type at the
very commencement of each titlepage, which
Halliwell-Phillipps considers a remarkable testimony to Shakespeare's popularity.

In June, 1607, Susannah, Shakespeare's oldest
daughter, was married to Dr. Hall, — a marriage
which must have been in every way agreeable to
the poet, as Dr. Hall was a man of education and
more than common ability. On the 31st of De-
cember in that year, Edmund Shakespeare was
buried at Southwark. He was the youngest child
of John Shakespeare; and though he was only a
player, and one of no great reputation, the bell was
tolled in his honour.

On the 21st of February, 1608, Elizabeth Hall
was born. She was the only child of her parents,
and on her all the ambitious hopes of Shakespeare
were thenceforward to rest.

Plays written by Shakespeare, or adapted by
him to the uses of the theatre, continued to follow
one another pretty rapidly. As soon as they were
performed, some publisher would get the consent

of the Master of the Revels to their publication.
The company, however, who wished to keep the
profits to themselves, would refuse; and any con-
scientious printer being obliged to yield to their
wishes, whatever plays were printed came to the
light in some dishonourable way.   In 1608
Thomas Pavior impudently published "The Yorkshire Tragedy" as having been written by William
Shakespeare, while Shakespeare and his company
were travelling along the southern coast.

In September of the same year Mary Arden,
the mother of Shakespeare, died; and her death
probably brought Shakespeare to Stratford, and
one of his friends took advantage of his presence.
On the 16th of October he was principal godfather
to William Walker, the son of one of the Stratford
aldermen.   Other business engaged him; he had
begun an action, afterwards decided in his favour,
against one John Addenbroke, but Addenbroke
disappearing, he was obliged to proceed against
a man named Horneby, who had stood bail for
him.   Thomas Greene, his solicitor, who was then
living at New Place, managed these affairs.

In 1609 appeared "Shake-speare's Sonnets, never
before Imprinted."   They were entered at Station-
ers' Hall, May 20.   The publisher, one Thorpe,
obtained these evidently from one of Shakespeare's

friends, — a certain W. H., to whom he dedicates the book. He can hardly express gratitude enough to this person, and he calls attention to Shakespeare's authorship by large capitals.

The same year Shakespeare's company took possession of Blackfriars'. This consisted of Heminges, Condell, Burbage, and himself.

In 1610 Shakespeare bought twenty acres of land of the Combes. Gilbert Shakespeare must have been a good manager, for Shakespeare accumulates land as rapidly as reputation.

In this year and in 1611 plays continued to pour from the press.

" The Tempest " was performed before King James and the Court, Nov. 1, 1611.

In 1612 Shakespeare was involved in a suit concerning his local tithes, some of the lessees failing in duty, and leaving Shakespeare and others to pay an unfair proportion. The income of his share of the tithes at this time was £60.

In the spring of 1613 "The Winter's Tale " was performed before Prince Charles, the Lady Elizabeth, and the Prince Elector Palatine.

On the 11th of September Shakespeare's name is found at Stratford, on a folio page of donors " towards the charge of prosecuting the better repayre of the highewaies."

It was now that some of Heywood's verses were
published with Shakespeare's name attached to
them, by a printer named Jaggard. "The author
I know much offended with M. Jaggard, that, unknown to him, presumed to make so bold with his
name," writes Heywood.

On the 4th of February, 1613, Shakespeare's
brother Richard died, at the age of thirty-nine.
Nothing is known of his life or story except that,
like Gilbert, he had probably never married.

A great deal has been written of those clos-
ing years when Shakespeare lived at Stratford,
released from every care save that of providing the
theatre with two plays a year, and enjoying an
ample income, with frequent visits from his London friends; but the interval of complete rest
must have been a very brief one.

From 1597, when he bought New Place, where
he laid out orchards and planted a mulberry,
Shakespeare probably resided at Stratford a part
of every year, and after the marriage of his daughter it is hardly likely that he personally appeared
upon the stage. In the "Conveyance," at the time
he bought one hundred and seven acres of the
Combes in 1602, he is called "William Shakespeare
of Stratford upon Avon." In 1608 he is spoken of
as "William Shakespeare, late an actor," and may

actually have left the stage some time before.
When he was taxed in Southwark in 1596, he
was probably living with his brother Edmund,
who died there in 1607, and was buried at St.
Saviour's, with a tolling of the "forenone bell."
After this date Shakespeare would have been still
more likely to pass every possible moment at
Stratford. He certainly looked closely after his
interests there after Gilbert's death in February,
1612. We do not know that he had ever had a
day's illness, and he might reasonably have looked
forward a quarter of a century. But the end was
already drawing near. In March he bought his
Blackfriars' estate in London at so extravagant a
price as to show that he was very anxious to pos-
sess it; but whether as a possible winter residence
for himself, or for some purpose connected with
the theatre, does not clearly appear. I am in-
clined to think that he bought it in the interest
of his theatrical friends, for a mortgage of £60 was
left upon it, and it was delivered to trustees, who
immediately leased it to one John Robinson. If
it were bought to protect the interest of his old
friends at Blackfriars', and in the hope that they
would soon take possession of it, this hope was
certainly disappointed.

It would seem as if he must have relinquished

his interest in the Globe before this time, as at the period of its destruction by fire, on the 29th of June, 1613, his name is nowhere mentioned in connection with it. "King Henry VIII." was on the stage at the moment, the part of the king being taken by Lowin, a very accomplished actor. This man was said to have been taught by Shakespeare. Lowin taught Davenant, and Davenant Betterton, so the traditions of Shakespeare's manner may have descended to our time.

Just before the theatre was burned, there was started at Stratford some miserable scandal concerning Susannah Hall and one Ralph Smith, which Dr. Hall thought proper to notice. The story was traced, and the man who set it afloat was summoned to the Ecclesiastical Court. Robert Whatcott, Shakespeare's friend, appeared for Susannah. Neither defendant nor proxy showed himself; and Lane, the slanderer, was formally excommunicated July 27, 1613. The story would be hardly worth repeating, except that it shows us how certainly any real peccadilloes of the poet or his family must have been preserved for us.

In 1614 the Corporation thought fit to send to New Place a quart of sack and another of claret, for the entertainment of a preacher sojourning there. This was a custom of the times.

In July John Combe died, and left to Shakespeare the handsome legacy of £5.

In the autumn of this year Shakespeare became involved in an unpopular movement, which did not do much credit to his insight. William Combe undertook to secure the enclosure of the common-fields, a measure which, if it had been successful, would have reduced the amount of taxes received by the Corporation, and also have diminished the number of labourers employed in the town. In various ways Combe influenced many persons, both rich and poor, to assist his purpose, and Shakespeare had been too long his friend to array himself in opposition. On the 23d of November the Corporation, evidently thinking that Shakespeare did not quite know what was doing, addressed a letter to him. Thomas Greene, Shakespeare's cousin and solicitor, and also the Stratford town clerk, was in London, where Shakespeare arrived on the 16th of November. The following extracts from Greene's diary are very curious, and contain the only account that exists of a personal interview with the poet: —

" 1. Jovis. 17 Nov. my cozen Shakspeare comyng yesterday to towne, I went to see him, how he did. He told me that they assured him they ment to inclose noe further than to Gospell

Bushe, and so upp straight (leaving out part of the Dyngles to the Field) to the gate in Clopton hedge, and take in Salisbury's peece; and that they mean in Aprill to survey the land, and then to gyve satisfaction and not before; and he and Mr. Hall say they think ther will be nothyng done at all.

"2. 23 Dec. A. hall. Letters wrytten, one to Mr. Manyring, another to Mr. Shakspear, with almost all the company's handes to eyther. I alsoe wrytte of myself to my cosen Shakspear the coppye of all our actes, and then also a not of the inconveniences would happen by the inclosure.

"3. 10 Januarii, 1614. Mr. Mannaryng and his agreement for me, with my cosen Shakspeare.

"4. 9 Jan. 1614. Mr. Replyngham 28 Octobris article with Mr. Shakspere, and then I was putt in by T. Lucas.

"5. Sept. (1615?) Mr. Shakspere told Mr. J. Greene that I was not abble to beare the enclosing of Welcombe."

The name of Mr. Replyngham may create some confusion. This gentleman was intending to enclose some land, and his "article" with Mr. Shakespeare pledged him to pay to William Shakespeare and Thomas Greene whatever *they* might lose by said enclosing.

5

Greene had returned to Stratford, Mr. Halliwell-Phillipps tells us, before the letter of the Corporation was written. The effort at enclosure was defeated, as it deserved to be.

The entry of September 5 contains the only recorded words of our great poet, and as such will always have a mournful interest for us.

The pleasant days went on for a few weeks. Jonson and Drayton came to see Shakespeare, and very likely went to the old inn where he had been accustomed to watch the antics of a "fool," that he might immortalize him in the company of Sly, Naps, Turf, and Pimpernell. The hilarity of the party had attracted the attention of the villagers, for when, in March, 1616, the poet was stricken with fever, the rumour ran that it came of too much drinking with his friends.

Considering the suddenness of this illness, it is a little singular that the draft of Shakespeare's last will had been made on the 16th of January preceding. His daughter Judith had been married to Thomas Queeney without a license on the 10th of February, and the pair were afterwards fined by the Ecclesiastical Court for the liberty taken. It does not appear that Shakespeare anticipated the marriage at the time the draft of his will was made. On the 25th of March his lawyer,

Francis Collins, was summoned, and the will has-
tily interlined to suit the altered circumstances,
and signed by Shakespeare. His mind was still
clear, for he suggested the interlineations himself,
and the two words, "by mee," are written in a
strong hand.

Judith received an ample marriage portion, but,
according to the customs of the time, it was upon
the poet's oldest child that the responsibility of
sustaining the family honours devolved, and to her
he devised the real estate he had been so long
and so steadily acquiring. Susannah Hall and her
husband were the executors. The law secured the
dowry of Shakespeare's wife to her use, and gave
her a life interest in New Place; and knowing
well the tender sympathy afterwards exhibited in
the epitaph inscribed upon her tomb, Shakespeare
doubtless felt himself safe in trusting his wife to
her daughter's care. This might have been made
necessary by the state of her health.

When the will was brought to Shakespeare's
bedside the alterations made were such as affection
suggested or the full sense required. Observing
that he had given to his daughter Susannah all
his silver plate, he took pains to mention that his
"broad silver gilt bowle" was to be given to Judith.
He remembered that his wife would want the

"second-best" bed, in addition to whatever the
law would give her, and he observed that the house
in Henley Street had not been properly secured
to his sister. The manner in which he provides
for "Joan Harte" suggests the idea that she had
remained in the Henley-Street house ever since her
father's death, perhaps supported by her brother's
purse. It was necessary also to add a clause re-
minding Susannah that "New Place" was given
to her especially to secure certain ends; among
them, perhaps, some special care of her mother.

In the first draft of the will Shakespeare had
given handsome legacies to the poor of Stratford, Thomas Russell, and Francis Collins. He
had given his sword to Thomas Combe, and certain sums in gold to William Walker, his godson,
as well as Anthony and John Nash. At the last
moment he leaves rings to Hamnet Sadler, William
Reynoldes, and his "fellows," Heminges, Burbage,
and Condell. Owing to the irregularity of the
paper, five witnesses signed it. It is a little
curious that in the copy of the will printed by
Theobald in 1767, "my *second*-best bed" reads
"*brown* best bed;" but as the reading has not
been followed it is doubtless an error.

Joan Harte's husband died on the 17th of April,
and on the 23d Shakespeare himself.

On the 25th the funeral was solemnized. His body was deposited in the chancel, the honorary resting-place of the owners of the tithes. Strange indeed that we know nothing of him who read the prayers at his grave, of the friends who gathered to do him honour, or the pall-bearers who bore the body to its rest!

Far away in Virginia (we were once told), for a long time sheltered by forest trees, was a stone commemorating one who died in the seventeenth century, — " one of the pall-bearers of William Shakespeare." Alas, that there was no truth in the legend!

A few years after the death of Shakespeare, certainly before the year 1623, a monument was erected to him in Stratford church. It is supposed to have been set up by Dr. Hall and his wife, but as it was made in London by Gerard Johnson, a well-known sculptor, whose place of business was near Blackfriars' Theatre, I cannot help thinking that it was far more likely to have been made to the order of his " fellowes " at the theatre, assisted by his personal friends. It was certainly ordered by some one not in the councils of the family, for it speaks of Shakespeare as having been placed " within this monument " by " envious Death," whereas his body rested in a simple grave some distance from the wall. If the Halls had erected the monument, Dr. Hall would probably have furnished the verses; and with his well-known Puritan tendencies we can hardly imagine him as rating Shakespeare's dramatic work so high as to say that with him "Quick nature died."

Gerard Johnson must have been perfectly familiar with the face and form of Shakespeare, as he went back and forth at Blackfriars'. He represented the poet with a cushion before him, a pen in his right hand, and his left resting on a roll of papers.

This bust is supposed to have been made after a mask or cast of the face taken after death by the artist, as was not uncommon at the time.

It is believed that the famous "Death Mask," a cast discovered in a private museum, is the original mask, as it bears the date of his death, 1616, inscribed upon it. It is so much nobler and sweeter than any existing likeness of him, it looks so much more as we would have liked Shakespeare to look, that we long to find it proved.

"The bust," says Wivell, "is fixed under an arch between two Corinthian columns of black marble, with gilded bases and capitals supporting the entablature. Above this, and surmounted by a

Death's head, are carved his arms. On each side
is a cherub in a sitting posture, one holding in his
hand a spade, and the other an inverted torch,
while one hand rests upon a skull."

The bust was at first coloured. The eyes were
hazel and the hair auburn, of the same colour as
that clinging to the "Death Mask." The dress
was a scarlet doublet, over which a loose black
gown without sleeves was thrown. The whole
figure has been two or three times repainted, and
has little interest now as a likeness of the poet.

On a tablet below the bust is the following
inscription :—

> "Judicio Pylum, genio Socratem, arte Maronem.
>   Terra tegit, populus mœret, Olympus habet.
>
> "Stay, Passenger, why goest thou by so fast ?
>   Read, if thou canst, whom envious Death hath placed
>   Within this monument : Shakespeare, with whom
>   Quick nature died, whose name doth deck this Tombe
>   Far more than cost ; sith all that he hath writ
>   Leaves living Art but page to serve his wit.
>
>   "Obiit Anno Domini, 1616,
>   Ætatis 53, die 23 April."

If we translate freely the two Latin lines we
have :—

> "Wise as the man of Pylos, inspired like Socrates, and with
>   the skill of Maro.
>   Earth covers, the people mourn, and Olympus holds him."

It has been said that Shakespeare died a Papist, — a rumour which simply meant, I suppose, that he did not die a Puritan. I am not a proper judge of the Latin verses of Shakespeare's time, but I risk little in saying that if any compromising Puritan had thought fit to write this epitaph he would hardly have made these over-strained and somewhat affected references to Nestor and Virgil. They sound much more like Ben Jonson than Dr. Hall.

Those who are of opinion that the grave of Shakespeare should be opened, draw pregnant conclusions from the spade in the cherub's hand, and the words " within this monument." If, however, these words had any cabalistic meaning, they would not point toward the grave, but toward some enclosure behind the panel of the monument itself.

Judith Shakespeare was the longest lived of the poet's family. Her three children died early. Her husband, Thomas Queeney, was a burgess and a chamberlain, and for some years a prosperous man. He eventually fell into idle ways, became bankrupt, and was supported by a brother in London. Judith died at Stratford in 1662.

Dr. Hall, Susannah's husband, was a skilful man, whose services were sought at great distances by many who did not approve of his Puritanism. He was a hot, impetuous person, continually quarrelling with the Corporation. He had sold his share of the tithes some time before his death, in 1635, but the Corporation did not refuse him the honour of lying beside the poet in the chancel. It is probably to his pen that we owe the epitaph on Anne Hathaway, who lived only seven years after her husband. She died Aug. 8, 1623, at the age of sixty-seven. In 1642 a surgeon named Cooke went to New Place to look at some books which Susannah Hall offered for sale. He saw that two of them were Latin manuscripts prepared by Dr. Hall himself for the press, but his widow refused to believe it. One of them, a portion of a medical diary, was afterwards translated into English, and published by Cooke.

On July 11, 1649, Susannah died, and on the gravestone a charming character is recorded : —

> " Witty above her sex, but that's not all :
> Wise to salvation was good Mistress Hall.
> Something of Shakspere was in *that*, but this
> Wholly of him with whom she's now in bliss,
> Then passenger, hast ne'er a tear
> To weep with her, that wept with all ?
> That wept, yet set herself to cheer
> Them up, with comforts cordial ?
> Her love shall live, her mercy spread
> When thou hast ne'er a tear to shed."

By this it will be seen that while Susannah inherited her wit from the poet, she owed "wisdom unto salvation" to the influence of the Puritan husband to whom she was now reunited. Bright intelligence, religious fervour, and warm sympathies may well have belonged to Shakespeare's oldest child.

Elizabeth Hall was the only grandchild of Shakespeare who lived long enough to marry, and the only child of her parents. She was married at the age of eighteen to a man of property in Stratford named Thomas Nash, fifteen years older than herself. They had no children. During the year 1643 she and her husband entertained Queen Henrietta Maria at New Place for three days. The Queen had come at the head of two thousand foot and a thousand horse to visit the town. Prince Rupert met her there, and the Corporation paid the expenses. It was a season of great festivity.

When she was left a widow twenty years after, Elizabeth was in her forty-third year, and she married a second time, her husband being a man of wealth and position from Northamptonshire, named John Barnard, who was afterwards knighted.

It is impossible not to feel an intense interest in any one who sustained personal relations with

Shakespeare. What would we not give to talk with any one who had talked with him ? For that reason, Dr. John Hall's

"Select Observations on English Bodies" possessed a great attraction for me. Mr. Halliwell-Phillipps, while admitting that it contains some notes on his own illnesses, and those of his wife and daughter, asserts that, as it contains nothing bearing upon Shakespeare, it is of no interest. By comparing the Doctor's notes upon the different members of his family, I found enough to make me feel thankful that none of Shakespeare's descendants through Elizabeth Hall should survive. Lady Barnard inherited her father's temperament; and the nervous affection of the face, which he subdued with so much difficulty in his daughter's youth, showed itself in him as soon as he was exhausted by his professional labours. Among other things, he ordered his "only daughter," as he writes with mournful pathos, to "eat nutmegs." This remedy for nervous restlessness is still used in rural regions; and a "cup of hot milk, well sugared, with half a nutmeg grated into it," is still considered, in country places, a good "night-cap" for those who sleep little.

Elizabeth died at the age of sixty-two, devising her property to kinsfolk and collateral relatives.

With her death, in 1670, ends our interest in the
property which Shakespeare so diligently accumulated for a posterity which was never to exist.
There is a great contrast between the plain stone
which covers Shakespeare's grave, with its homely
inscription, and the elaborate monument set in the
wall not five paces from it. In Shakespeare's time
it was customary to hire a grave for a short time
only, and then remove the bones of the dead to
the common charnel-house. In this way, nine
years after the great poet's death, the celebrated
Puritan minister, John Robinson, was buried in
the church at Leyden, where his wife hired a
"three-months" grave. An account of his funeral
was preserved; and as it was impossible to find any
traces of interment, scholars were much perplexed
until a younger brother of Charles Sumner made
a thorough search in the old records and discovered the facts. As late as the beginning of the
eighteenth century, a traveller named Ireland reported the offensive condition of the Stratford
charnel-house; and it was probably in loving
recognition of some feeling that Shakespeare had
expressed, that the famous "curse" was set upon
his grave.

William Hall, who visited Shakespeares' grave
in 1694, and whose manuscript account of what

he found is preserved in the Bodleian Library, states that, to carry out the desire expressed in the lines engraved upon the poet's tombstone, they had laid his body seventeen feet below the surface, where one would think that by this time identification would be impossible.

Seven years after Shakespeare's death his two friends, Heminges and Condell, to each of whom he had left a ring, brought out his Plays. These men were, like himself, proprietors of the Globe and Blackfriars', and the owners of all Shakespeare's Plays. If Shakespeare had ever wanted to print them, he could not have done it without buying the manuscripts back; but when he died, he was probably in the full vigour of authorship, and had little thought that the time had come when he should undertake it. If his friends expected to make money by giving them to the reading public, the task was quite as much undertaken to "keep his memory alive."

We cannot doubt that these two friends knew who wrote the plays. Betterton "more than once assured Gildon that the first folio contained all those [plays] that were truely his." Betterton had been an officer at "Blackfriars'," and knew what the players thought. There are several contemporaneous statements as to the carelessness and rapidity with which Shakespeare wrote. That Ben Jonson knew Shakespeare as the author of the Plays, his Eulogy and the verses inscribed beneath the Droeshout portrait certainly show. It is not my intention to enter on any discussion of the Bacon *v.* Shakespeare controversy; but I hope these pages will prove that we know as much of Shakespeare as we could expect to know of a man who lived three hundred years ago.

As to the preservation of his manuscripts, they were probably worn out in the service of those who had bought them before the First Folio was printed; and his letters and private papers may well have perished in the great fire at Stratford, in the years of the plague, or in the two great fires which finally swept off the face of London every building that was connected with his history, with the one exception already indicated.

As to his social station, it was that to which New England is indebted for her best citizens, — for the Winthrops, the Peabodys, the Rogerses, the Lawrences, and the Appletons; for when not described as soldiers or clergymen, these emigrants were described as *yeomen.*

That John Shakespeare was ever seriously embarrassed, — or more embarrassed than any man may be who mortgages one piece of property to buy another, — admits of doubt. That he is constantly mentioned as "Mr. John Shakespeare," shows the consideration in which he was held. As to William Shakespeare's character, it is not often that we have so graphic a portrait of any man as that preserved of him by Ben Jonson in his "Discoveries;" and no one could apply that portrait to the well-known features of Francis Bacon without a supreme sense of the ridiculous : —

"I remember the players have often mentioned, as an honour to Shakespeare, that, in his writing, whatsoever he penned, he never blotted a line. My answer hath been, would he had blotted a thousand, which they thought a malevolent speech. I had not told posterity this, but for their ignorance, who choose that circumstance to commend their friend by, wherein he most faulted, and to justify mine own Candour, for I loved the man, and do honor his memorie on this side idolatrie as much as any. He was indeed honest, and of an open and free nature; had an excellent phantasie, brave notions, and gentle expressions, wherein he flowed with that facility that sometime it was necessarie he should be stoped. His wit was in his own power; would the rule of it had been so too."

"Many times he fell into those things would
not escape laughter, as when he said of Cesar, —
one speaking to him : 'Cesar, thou dost me wrong,'
he replied, 'Cesar did never wrong but with just
cause,' and such like, which were ridiculous; but
he redeemed his vices with his virtues. There
was ever more in him to be praysed than to be
pardoned."

This criticism, which few close students of human nature will be found to accept, is here quoted
to show how peremptorily Ben Jonson claimed the
Plays of Shakespeare for the man he knew and
loved. When he rendered the works of Francis
Bacon into Latin, it was not because he loved *him*
"as much as any this side idolatrie."

There are few personal relics of Shakespeare
which can be authenticated. It is singular that
not a piece of his silver is known to exist. In
Philadelphia, Horace Howard Furness possesses a
pair of gauntlets which once belonged to the poet.
When Garrick was preparing for the Jubilee at
Stratford, in 1769, John Ward, an actor, and the
maternal grandfather of Mrs. Siddons, wrote him
a letter accompanying a gift of a pair of buckskin
gauntlets worked with gold thread. These gloves,
Ward asserted, were given him as a compliment
after his performance of " Othello " at Stratford, in

1746, which was undertaken to assist in repairing Shakespeare's monument. The donor was a certain William Shakespeare, glazier, who said he was descended from a cousin of the poet's father. We have a pleasant and early reminiscence of one of Shakespeare's great-nephews, who said that when he was a boy, the children of the family used to dress up in the poet's disused garments. Ward was at this time a very old man, and had probably forgotten some of the details, for they are not quite credible as they stand in the first volume of the private correspondence of Garrick. In 1769, however, Ward gave these gloves in full faith to Garrick, who left them in his will to Mrs. Siddons, who was Ward's granddaughter. Mrs. Siddons gave them to her daughter, Mrs. George Combe, and Mrs. Combe in her turn presented them to Fanny Kemble, from whose keeping they naturally passed into the library of her friend, Horace Howard Furness, the Shakespearean scholar.

The marvellous industry of Shakespeare has left its own proof in " Venus and Adonis," " The Rape of Lucrece," the Sonnets, and the thirty-seven wonderful Plays. If it were a miracle that such a man could exist, it was still more of a miracle that this man met acceptance and reward in his lifetime. It is certain that he was idolized by the people, sought by the nobility, petted by the Court, and admired by both Elizabeth and James, in spite of his freedom from pedantry. It was no miracle that he accumulated property,—that was the natural result of industry and thrift; but that he kept so high a tone in all he wrote, in an age of great coarseness and ribaldry, and kept it without losing popular favour, argues a miraculous charm in the man himself, such as Ben Jonson attributes to him.

The following anecdote seems worth preserving, in view of Ben Jonson's opinion of the poet's scholarship. Shakespeare was godfather to a child of Ben Jonson. After the baptism he was standing pensively apart, and Jonson went up to him, saying, "What's the matter, Will?" "Why, Ben," replied the poet, "I was only thinking what gift I might bestow upon my godson. I have it! I will give him a dozen Latten spoones, and thou, Ben, shalt translate them!" This little legend reads as if Shakespeare had heard of the "small Latine and lesse Greeke." *Latten* spoons were made of pewter, or what is now called German Silver.

Those who take no interest whatever in what is called the "Baconian" controversy have often been heard to wonder that we have no evidence of any acquaintance between Bacon and Shakespeare,— the two greatest intellects of their time.

These men must have crossed each other's path continually; but one was primarily a poet and an actor, the other a statesman and a scientist. Shakespeare shows in his Plays that he sprung from the people; he cared for the people, — their liberties, their rights, and their interests. Perhaps he had at first some desire to take a practical part in politics, but the death of Essex made this impossible; and never after Essex died could a man of his upright dealing and tender heart have clasped hands with Lord Bacon. It might have been Bacon's duty to withdraw from Essex; it could never have been his duty, except as a mean effort towards self-preservation, to become his public prosecutor, still less to garble the records of his examination before their publication. After this, any intimacy with Shakespeare would have been impossible. After Bacon's return to England in 1580, he was in such a position that, unless at the playhouse, he would hardly have encountered Shakespeare.

Whoever wishes to understand the popularity of the thirty-seven Plays, to ascertain the manner in which editions, spurious or other, were put forth year after year, and how, when it was impossible to prevent unscrupulous persons from printing, Shakespeare himself was obliged to revise and amplify them, must consult the records furnished by Halliwell-Phillipps. Such a theme does not suit this brief biography.

It is supposed that Shakespeare devoted a good deal of time to classical study during the last years of his life, for the three Roman plays show so intimate an acquaintance, not only with Roman manners, but with Roman diction and modes of thought, as to make this probable.

Fifty years after Shakespeare's death, the Rev. John Ward became vicar of Stratford. He found the town full of traditions respecting Shakespeare, of whom he apparently knew nothing. Shakespeare's granddaughter was then alive, but she was at Abington Manor, near Northampton. Some of us would have gone to see her, to find out all that she could tell, but the new vicar was not that sort of man. He was astonished to find everybody talking about Shakespeare. He heard a great many foolish legends, but not a scandalous word concerning the poet's relation to his wife, nor his treatment of her in his will. He wrote down what he heard, and made a memorandum to the effect that he must study up the Plays, in order to be able to talk about them!

From the hour that Anne Hathaway married Shakespeare, to the hour of her death, we hear no

word of her. The common English law of the
time justified Shakespeare's will. Without any
word of his, it gave *her* a life-interest in all that
he had inherited, and a life-interest in New Place,
as he held it by direct conveyance. Dr. Hall and
his wife had probably been living at New Place
for some years, and her life went on after the
poet's death in the same tranquil manner that it
had done during his life. She expressed but one
wish, — to be laid near her husband, — and that
was not regarded. In deference to the feeling
indicated by the words, —

> " Good friends, for Jesus' sake forbeare,"

she was not interred in the same grave. I do
not know that the inscription upon her grave-
stone, said to have been written in Latin by Dr.
Hall, has ever been translated. It is much better
verse than was common. It scans well, and seems
to me to have both beauty and strength. It is her
daughter who addresses her, and the following is a
literal translation of the lines : —

> " My life, thy breast, thy milk thou gavest, mother.
> Ah me, for gifts so great I give a stone!
> Would that some good angel might lift that stone,
> And thy spirit come forth like the body of Christ !
> But prayers avail not. Come quickly, O Jesus,
> Though shut in the tomb, she shall seek the stars."

THE FAMILY OF RICHARD
SHAKESPEARE.

THE FAMILY OF RICHARD SHAKESPEARE.

RICHARD SHAKESPEARE of Snitterfield had sons, Henry and John.

John married Mary Arden, 1557, and had a large family, of whom only William, Joan Harte, Richard, Gilbert, and Edmund seem to have lived to maturity.

Joan Harte had several sons.

Richard died unmarried three years before his brother.

Gilbert went into some business in London, but returned to Stratford, and acted as agent for his brother. He is supposed to have died in 1612.

Edmund was a player, who died in Southwark, and was buried at St. Saviour's, Dec. 31, 1607.

THE FAMILY OF WILLIAM SHAKESPEARE.

THE FAMILY OF WILLIAM SHAKESPEARE.

WILLIAM SHAKESPEARE, born 1564, married Anne Hathaway, born 1556, in 1582. Anne Hathaway's family is not known certainly. They had

Susannah, born 1583, married Dr. John Hall, 1607, died 1649.

Hamnet, twin to Judith, born 1585, died 1596.

Judith, twin to Hamnet, born 1585, married Thomas Queeney, 1616, died 1662.

Susannah and John Hall had Elizabeth Hall, born 1608, married, first, Thomas Nash, 1626; and second, Sir John Barnard, 1649. She died without issue, 1670, when the poet's lineage became extinct.

The orthography of all proper names used in these pages is uncertain and constantly varied. I prefer Queeney to Quiney, as it indicates the Norman origin and pronunciation.

THE PERSONAL CHARACTER OF SHAKESPEARE.

THE PERSONAL CHARACTER OF
SHAKESPEARE.

" Lilies that fester smell far worse than weeds."
SHAKESPEARE.

MR. HALLIWELL-PHILLIPPS follows the example
of other authors in constantly reiterating that
nothing which is to be found in Shakespeare's
Plays can be considered as in any degree in-
dicative of his personal character. I cannot for
one moment admit this. I am well aware that a
very bad man may write eloquently in defence of
virtue, but the *how* he writes of it will inevitably
betray his want of sympathy with it.

It does not trouble me to know that after a
merry bout with the " sippers " of Bidford, Shakespeare might have found himself obliged to pass
a night under the old tree on the high-road, which
was called, until its decayed condition made it
necessary to remove it, " Shakespeare's canopy."

Excessive drinking was hardly considered in
his time a bad habit, certainly it was by very few
regarded as a vice ; but if this anecdote be true,

7

still we know from all the evidences of his life that Shakespeare was not a drunkard. Honesty and thrift distinguished him, as every intelligent reader of the advice of Polonius to Laertes would expect.

As to his personal reserve and chastity, united as they must have been to a natural love of fun and a most genial disposition, we find the proof of it in the exquisite sensitiveness which he shows to those traits in his women. George Gordon Byron could never have been the creator of Cordelia, Portia, or Miranda.

I think no author of his time could have treated the voluptuous story of "Venus and Adonis" as Shakespeare treated it. All through the hot air of its passion a fresh, pure breeze of something higher trembles, and I am astonished that more has not been made of this point by critics. His "Lucrece" was considered in his own time "a perfect exposition of a woman's chastity," and that exposition a gross man could neither have made nor understood.

Very delicate and discriminating observations on character abound in his Plays and Sonnets; and such qualities as they show do not belong to those who have blunted their own perceptions by degrading habits.

Personally he would have been much better known to the world if he had carried his family to London. In Stratford he could have found little to induce him to enter general society, and his time must have been well occupied with business and composition.

He wrote as a bird sings, and therefore the ethics of his Plays are the natural evolution of their dramatic purpose, but were never intentionally included in his plan.

In politics he seems to me to have been from the beginning the unconscious mouth-piece of a very liberal party. The death of Essex was perhaps a not unneeded lesson, and the ultimate purposes of the earl must have been a startling surprise.

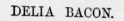

DELIA BACON.

DELIA BACON.

IT has been the custom of sincere students of Shakespeare's life who believe, as I do, in his identity, to ignore wholly what is now called the " Baconian Theory of the Origin of the Plays;" and by alluding to it, I may have offended the taste of more than one reader.

It seems to me, however, that the literature connected with the subject has now reached such proportions that wholly to ignore it is at once cowardly and absurd; but I have still another reason for alluding to it, personal to myself.

I knew and loved Delia Bacon. She was a woman of the rarest personal gifts, of whom no suitable record remains, if we except the wonderful story of the ecclesiastical trial, written by Catherine Beecher, in " Truth Stranger than Fiction."

A terrible personal experience warped her mind soon after she entered upon her historical studies. The warp was shown when a nature essentially of the noblest turned mean and suspicious. To obtain means to pursue her Shakespearean researches,

she gave lectures on History in several American
cities, among others in Boston, where men like
Ralph Waldo Emerson, William Henry Channing,
and many of their compeers found delight in lis-
tening to her.

Even now, it is only necessary to close my eyes,
to see once more that graceful form which always
suggested the priestess of Apollo, to hear again the
vibrant voice which penetrated to one's inmost soul.
After she had perfected her theory, she never com-
municated it fully to any one ; she seemed to fear
that her laurels would be stolen if she did so.   In
the month of January, 1856, there appeared in
"Putnam's Monthly," an article entitled,

" William Shakspere and his Plays, An
Inquiry concerning them."

This article was the first public utterance of Delia
Bacon, and then and there began this famous controversy.   I forget what I thought of it then, except that I did not in any wise agree with it ; but
as I go back to it, it grieves me bitterly, its coarseness and flippancy seem so unworthy of, and so
unlike, my friend.   Other articles were promised ;
but a good deal of literary indignation had been
aroused, and the publishers thought proper to decline them.   Miss Bacon then went to England
and to Stratford, and before long her very remarka-

ble critical volume called "The Philosophy of Shakspere's Plays," was issued, and introduced by Hawthorne. Before she left this country she discussed her method of publication with Mr. Emerson and myself, and probably with many others. She said that she drew her evidences of Francis Bacon's authorship from two sources, the internal and the external. She found them in the Plays themselves, and outside of the Plays, in history. She wished to publish in two large octavo volumes. She had enough of each sort of material to fill a volume; which should she print first?

I said: "The facts, by all means, if you have them."

Mr. Emerson said: "Your inductions, by all means; and then clinch them with your facts."

It is hardly necessary to say that she followed Emerson's advice.

After her most unhappy death, — a death precipitated by sorrow, loneliness, privation, and consequent despair, — I wrote to her brother and asked permission to examine her papers, with a view to preparing some memorial of a life which, in spite of some mistakes, had been exceptionally noble.

Permission was refused; and as her family had not the slightest sympathy with her later pursuits, it is possible that all her papers have been destroyed. They would undoubtedly have been very valuable to literary people, for she was an indefatigable and zealous copyist.

Mr. Emerson wished very much to review her "Philosophy of the Plays." He held the very highest estimate of the critical ability and wonderful insight which her book displayed. He came to me once to ask if I could suggest any volumes which would assist him to illustrate her purpose. He said that he could not have the "seeing eye;" she found so much, and he so little.

But, after all this, the reader must be reminded that Delia Bacon formed her theory before Mr. Halliwell-Phillipps's researches had begun; before Shakespeare emerged from the mists of Blackfriars' and the Globe, and stood before us as a well-known citizen of no small use in his time in other ways than as a

"Maker of playes."

A HISTORY OF THE ACCUMULATIONS

OF

JOHN AND WILLIAM SHAKESPEARE

FROM 1550 TO 1616.

To this I add a detailed account of the application for a
"coat of armour." I consider Mr. Halliwell-Phillipps the highest
authority in all that concerns the life of William Shakespeare.
When I differ from him it is where I think that in his anxiety
concerning the more important points, he has overlooked the
obvious bearing of many minor admissions.

ACCUMULATIONS OF JOHN AND WILLIAM SHAKESPEARE.

JOHN SHAKESPEARE was born at Snitterfield about the year 1530, for we are to suppose that he must have been of age when he went to Stratford.

His father Richard must have had a well-kept farm under the squires of Arden, for in 1543 Thomas Atwoode, of Stratford, leaves to Richard Shakespeare, by will, "foure oxen then in his keeping."

In 1550 John had left home; and in 1556, by the purchase of two houses in Stratford, one being in Greenhill, the other the famous Henley-Street property, he had provided himself with premises where a family could reside, and wool, skins, and other farm produce be sold.

In 1557 he married Mary Arden, the daughter of Robert Arden, Squire of Asbyes. She had received from her father, who died about a year before her marriage, a farm at Snitterfield, a house with sixty acres of land, and all appurtenances, at Wilmecote, called Asbyes, and a third of the farm tenanted by her husband's father, Richard Shakespeare.

Stratford took note of John Shakespeare's circumstances, and for twelve years he rose steadily through all the offices in the gift of the Corporation, till in 1569 he became high bailiff and mayor of Stratford. It has sometimes been asserted that it was the growing wealth and ambition of the poet which led his father to apply for a "coat of armour," but this is a mistake. It was in 1569, when William Shakespeare was only five years old, that, stimulated partly by a desire to keep up the Arden estate, and partly by the wish to keep alive the memory of honours conferred by Henry VII. upon his grandfather after the battle of Bosworth, John Shakespeare applied for his grant. The grant was made by Robert Cooke Clarencieux, king-at-arms, and confirmed by William Dethick Garter, principal king-at-arms.

In 1575 he purchased two houses of Edmund and Emma Hall in Stratford.

In 1578, probably to raise money for the purchase of outlying farms, to which allusion is made in the papers describing William Shakespeare's "inheritances," he mortgaged Asbyes.

In 1578 he became bondsman for Richard Hathaway, which indicates that *after* this mortgage he was supposed to be in good circumstances. This year he was "taxed one half," which seems to me to indicate, not that he had grown poor, but that he had removed beyond the limits of the parish.

In 1579 he sold to Robert Webbe the two Arden messuages at Snitterfield. In this year he is styled a yeoman, and is not "taxed" at all. The "taxes" referred to are not "tithes" or taxes upon his houses in Stratford, but his poor rate, — his share of the expenses proper to the parish.

When, in 1569, John Shakespeare applied for a "coat of armour," there is little doubt, I think, that he intended to remove from town and lead the life of a country squire. To do this, capital was necessary, and on that account he was at last obliged to mortgage Asbyes. His wife's brother-in-law, Edmund Lambert, took an unfair advantage of his circumstances, and when he was ready to lift the mortgage, in 1580, the home to which Mary Arden had expected to return was not open to her; Lambert refused the money.

In 1586, in a process for debt against one John Shakespeare, the sergeant-at-arms reports that there is "nothing to distrain upon." If this entry actually concerns the poet's father, I consider it another proof of non-residence, — there was noth-

ing to distrain upon within the borough. If he
had come to absolute want, why did he not mortgage or sell the Stratford property which his son
inherited ?   In this year he was removed from the
Corporation for non-attendance. This is another
proof of non-residence. Bishopton and Welcombe,
where the poet inherited property of which we
have no account, and which may have been part
of that bestowed by Henry VII. upon his ancestor, were within the limits of Stratford parish,
and beyond the borough.   Later, John is mentioned as one of nine men who do not come to
church for fear of being arrested for debt, — another proof of non-residence. If he lived in
the town he could be arrested any day.

In 1587 it was arranged, with the consent of
William Shakespeare, that, on cancelling the
mortgage and paying £20, the heir of Edmund
Lambert should receive an absolute title to the
estate of Asbyes.   The poet had been in London for five years.   He had probably left his
family in the Henley-Street house, and if John
Shakespeare removed to the country they were
doubtless left behind.   When the poet returned
to London, if he went abroad, as I think, he felt
secure that the best thing had been done for his
father's interests ; but the arrangement was never

carried out. In close connection with the entries
that concern John Shakespeare in the Corporation
books, appears the name of Robert Bratt. When
Bratt is to be taxed, the entry is: "Nothing in this
place;" and immediately following is another:
"Every alderman shall be taxed to pay weekly
toward the relief of the poor, fourpence, saving
John Shaxpeare and Robert Bratt, who shall not
be taxed to pay anything." Are we not justified
in thinking that the exemption was the result of
non-residence in both cases?

In 1596 the poet is taxed in Southwark, where
he was probably living with his younger brother
Edmund; and his father, having rallied from the
unfortunate circumstances into which the mortgage
had plunged him, applied again for his "coat of
armour." Asbyes was in chancery; but the
heralds report that he showed a previous patent,
and made a memorandum on the grant that he
had been chief officer of Stratford; "that he hath
lands and tenements of good wealth, and substance
five hundred pounds; that he married a daughter
and heir of Arden, a gentleman of worship." The
next year a bill is filed for the recovery of Asbyes.
There was no want of money then, for William is
buying arable land at Shottery, and the Corporation
would be glad to have him bid for the tithes.

Mary Arden had expected to leave her inheritance to her son; but as this expectation looked less and less likely to be realized, she naturally desired that some trace of her inheritance should survive in the "coat of armour;" and in 1599, when the poet was already famous, John Shakespeare petitions for the right to "impale the arms of Arden of Wellingcote," *which was granted.*

All this had not been done without stirring the wrath of those gentry of "wealth and ability" who had sustained Edmund Lambert in his unfair dealing. Charges were brought by Ralph Brooke, a York herald, against Garter and Clarencieux, that they had wrongfully given arms to twenty-three persons, and among them was John Shakespeare. The reply of the "kings," made upon the 10th of May, 1602, is as follows: "As for the speare in the bend, . . . the person to whom it was granted hath borne magistracy, and was justice of the peace at Stratford upon Avon. He married the daughter and heir of Arden, and was able to maintain that estate." John Shakespeare had now been dead for six months; but the reason why the poet thought fit to pursue the matter is easy to see. Behind Robert Brooke he saw the gentlemen of the county angered, perhaps, by the "impalement of the arms of Arden," and among these he had good reason to think he saw Sir Thomas Lucy, or his representative. The discontent of the county gentlemen had been growing ever since 1596; and it was an insult to his mother, which Shakespeare resented in the only personality of an unpleasant nature that we can trace to his pen. Some time between 1596 and July, 1600, Shakespeare had undoubtedly written that passage in the opening of the "Merry Wives of Windsor," which the critics have found so mysterious. The Welshman's scornful jest about the "dozen white *looses*," which "do become an *old* coat well," was a witty revenge. It is significant that the whole scene is a sneer at heraldic honours. The county gentry had sneered at the *new* honours granted to John Shakespeare's family. The pronunciation of the period gave the poet a chance to retort by a fling at the older pedigrees. The heralds had had ample time to come to a decision between 1596 and 1602. The falcon which was granted to Shakespeare as a crest was one of the badges of Edward IV., the father-in-law of Henry VII., and carried, like the Stuart lion, by special favour.

The facts of this application for a "grant of armour," extending from 1569 to 1602, dispose finally of the story of John Shakespeare's excessive poverty. They show that John Shakespeare

looked upon himself neither as a butcher, nor a
glover, nor a wool-stapler, but as a gentleman
sprung from the English yeomanry, anxious to
secure to his son whatever benefit might spring
from that acknowledged position.   We can hardly
think the poet himself cared much for heraldic
honours ; but we like to think of him as sustaining the application, because his father made it in
the face of a pronounced social opposition.   There
is a certain pleasant audacity in the motto he
bore, —

"NOT WITHOUT RIGHT."

As John Shakespeare left no will, we do not
know exactly in what way his property passed to
his son, or whether he took possession of any part
of it before his father's death.   A side light is
thrown upon the matter by a deed of covenant,
dated 1639, made to levy a fine on a resettlement
of the Shakespeare estate after the death of the
poet's son-in-law, Dr. Hall.   After rehearsing all
the well-known properties of Shakespeare, the
conveyance goes on to speak of "land, arable,
meadowe and pasture, with thappurtenances lying and being in the towns, hamblets, villages,
feildes, and groundes of Stratford upon Avon,
Old Stratford, Bishopton, and Welcombe, or any
of them in the said countie of Warwicke, which

heretofore were the *inheritance* of William Shakspere, gent., deceased."

This may point to the investments which led
John Shakespeare to mortgage Asbyes and sell out
at Snitterfield; or to the endowments of Henry
VII.; and also shows that no embarrassment had
existed sufficient to deprive the son of any portion
of the inheritance.

In the month of May, 1602, William Shakespeare is recognized as a resident of Stratford.
As such he buys one hundred and seven acres of
land from the Combes, which are delivered to his
brother Gilbert in his absence.   In 1597, five
years before, he had bought New Place and fitted
it up for his family.   If my theory of his life is
correct, his wife and children removed from the
Henley-Street wool-shop about 1598, leaving Joan
Harte in possession of the house.   Her mother
must have remained there until her death in
1608.

On the 28th of September, 1602, Shakespeare
bought a cottage and garden opposite New Place,
from one Walter Getly; in 1603 he bought a
messuage, with barns, gardens, and orchards, from
one Hercules Underhill; and from 1599 to 1612
his interest in the theatres in London was steadily
increasing.   He probably owned the wardrobes

and properties also, as we see by their valuation when they were parted with. The Globe was open in the summer, and Blackfriars' in the winter.

Shakespeare's technical residence must have been in Stratford from the time of his purchase of New Place, although he was probably absent six months out of every year until he sold out of the theatres. On March 11, 1613, Shakespeare made his last purchase, evidently entered upon to accommodate his old friends at Blackfriars', where he had not appeared as an actor since 1604, and in which he had some years since ceased to be a proprietor. Some property, which they were not able at the moment to buy, and the possession of which may have been essential to their interests, was bought at a price so heavy that Shakespeare could hardly have purchased it for himself. It was sold by one Henry Walker to Shakespeare and certain trustees. It was mortgaged to Walker the day after the purchase, and after his death the trustees accounted for it to his heirs.

In this sketch I have taken for granted the removal of John Shakespeare from the borough of Stratford, and the occupation of the Henley-Street house, or rather the half of it called the wool-shop, by William Shakespeare and his family. Should

I be mistaken in my inferences, the publication of them will only stimulate inquiry in new directions; but I think the fact of John Shakespeare's removal very clear.

As to Shakespeare's residence in Henley Street, my own suspicion of it is strengthened by an inference which will be found on another page;[1] but I will introduce it here.

In a conveyance of premises adjoining the birthplace in Henley Street, July 20, 1609, the following paragraph occurs : —

" between the tenemente of Thomas Hornbie on the easte parte and the tenemente *late* of William Shakspere on the weaste part."

On this Mr. Halliwell-Phillipps remarks : —

" Although no doubt the result of a mere clerical oversight, it should be noticed that, in the description of the parcels, *the word 'late,'* before the poet's name, is *interpolated.*"

But in a later conveyance of the same premises, dated Jan. 22, 1613, occurs the following : —

" betweene the tenemente of Thomas Hornebye on the easte parte and a tenemente *late William Shakspere* on the weaste parte."

Now, it is not likely that a clerical error should be repeated at the distance of more than four

[1] See p. 181.

years, not even if the clerk were actually copying the description of the parcels from the older conveyance. What then does the word "late" mean? Shakespeare was not dead; he had not sold the Henley-Street house. It must mean that, until he went to New Place, he and his family had lived there when in Stratford. It is possible he had leased it of his father; but if John Shakespeare had lived in it at the time of his death in 1601, it would have been much more natural for the clerk to write,

"late of John Shakspere."

Shakespeare's connection with the Theatres briefly stated.

He went to London in 1585.

Remained certainly till 1587.

Is not heard of again till 1592.

Next to Burbage, he was the largest proprietor of Blackfriars' in 1605.

A proprietor of the Globe, — constructed in 1600, — but not probably at the time of his death.

APPENDIX.

IN THE "CENTURIE OF PRAYSE,"

DR. INGLEBY FINDS

One hundred and eighty-five references to Shakespeare between 1592 and 1693. Of these *fifty-seven* were made during his lifetime. Many of these were the words of the most eminent of his contemporaries or their immediate successors, such as Spenser and Jonson, Milton, Dryden, and Cowley. Others were made in manuscript and by obscure persons.

THE "CENTURIE OF PRAYSE," BY DR. C. M. INGLEBY. LONDON, 1874.

HE quotes *eight different opinions* by Ben Jonson.

Robert Burton, 1624, says: "Venus ran out to meet her rose-cheeked Adonis, as an elegant Poet of ours has set her out."

Richard James, in 1625, tells us of the offence given by Shakespeare's use of the name of Sir John Oldcastle and his substitution of that of Falstaff.

Thomas Robinson, in 1630, describing the life of a monk, says: "After supper it is usual for him to read a little of 'Venus and Adonis' or some such scurrilous book."

John Taylor, in 1630, mentions Shakespeare as the peer of Spenser: "Spenser and Shakespeare did in Art excel."

Robert Southwell, 1594: —

> "Still finest wits are stilling Venus' Rose ;
> In paynim toyes the sweetest veins are spent."

Robert Tofte, in 1598, praises and criticises "Love's Labour's Lost."

Richard Barnefield, 1598, writes: —

> " And Shakspere, thou whose honey-flowing vaine
> Pleasing the world thy praises doth obtaine."

Walter Cope, in 1594, writes to Lord Cranbourne that " ' Love's Labour Lost' is to be played at the Earl of Southampton's, which for wit and humor will please the Queen exceedingly."

John Marston, in the "Scourge of Villainie," 1599, writes of Shakespeare : —

> " He writes, he rails, he jests, he courts (what not ?)
> And all from out his huge long scrapèd stocke
> Of well penned playes."

George Peele, in 1607, in "Merrie Conceited Jests" mentions "Venus and Adonis."

Louis Machin, 1608, the same.

Thomas Heywood, 1607, praises "Venus and Adonis."

In a *Preface* to "Troilus and Cressida," printed in 1609, it is said : "So much and such savored salt of wit is in his Commedies, that they seeme to be born in that sea which brought forth Venus."

A Manuscript Journal of the *Duke of Wurtemberg* says, April 30, 1610 : "They play the 'Moor of Venice' at the Globe."

Sir William Drummond says: " *Ben Jonson,* in 1618, said: ' William Shakspere wanted art and sometimes sense, since his men suffered shipwreck in Bohemia a hundred miles from any sea.' "

William Basse, in a manuscript of 1622, writes :

> " Sleep, brave Tragedian, Shakspere, sleep alone,
> In this uncarvèd marble of thine own.
> Thy unmolested rest and unshared cave
> Possesse as lord not tenant to thy grave,[1]
> That unto others, it may counted be
> Honour hereafter to be laid by thee."

Prefixed to the Second Folio of 1632 is this line : —

> " Rare Shakspere to the life thou dost behold."

I. M. S. prefixed to Second Folio, 1632, these lines : —

> "Shakspere shall breathe and speak with
> Laurel crowned which never fades."

William Payne, writing in 1642, says: " Shakspere's plays are better printed than most Bibles."

Aston Cokaine, in 1632, mentions Shakespeare as the peer of Jonson and Beaumont and Fletcher.

Shakespeare is quoted by William Rowley in 1632.

[1] An allusion evidently to the practice, heretofore alluded to, of *renting* graves.

William Habington, in 1634, cries : "A health to Shakspere's ghost !"

Thomas Heywood, in 1635, writes in the "Hierarchie of the Blessed Angels :" —

> " Mellifluous Shakspere, whose enchanting quill
> Commanded mirth or passion, was but Will."

Owen Feltham, in 1638, speaks of Shakespeare as the "chief gem in the crown of the stage."

Richard West, in 1638, says : "Shakspere may make grief merrie."

James Mervyn, in 1638, writes of Shakespeare's mirth.

In a "Banquet of Jests," 1639, we read that "Stratford is remarkable for the birth of the famous William Shakspere."

Thomas Bancroft, in 1639, says : —

> " Thou hast so used thy pen, or shook thy speare,
> That Poets startle nor thy wit come neare."

In a funeral song on Lady Helen Branch by *Sir William Harbert,* 1594, Shakespeare is rebuked for going into foreign countries for the subjects of his verse.

An edition of his *Poems,* 1640, has appended to it : —

> " Sleep then, rich soul of numbers, whilst poor we
> Enjoy the profits of thy legacy."

In 1636 *Sir John Suckling* wrote a "Supplement
to some of Shakspere's verses;" also the lines:—

> " The sweat of Johnson's learned brain,
>   And gentle Shakspere's easier strain."

James Shirley, in 1642, writes:—

> "To Shakspere comes whose mirth did once beguile
>   Dull hours; and buskined made even sorrow smile."

And again, in 1647, writing to Pembroke and
Montgomery, *Shirley* calls them "patrons to
the flowing compositions of the sweet swan of
Avon."

In "Mercurius Britannicus," some one writes,
1644, of " Ben Jonson and his *uncle* Shakspere"!

Sir John Denham writes to John Fletcher in
1647:—

> " When Jonson, Shakspere, and thyself did sit
>   And swayed in the triumvirate of wit."

Sir George Bucke, in 1647, writes:—

> "Let Shakspere, Chapman, and applauded Ben
>   Weare the eternal merit of their pen."

J. Birkenhead, in a eulogy prefixed to the first
edition of Beaumont and Fletcher, writes, 1647:

> " Brave Shakspere flowed, yet had his ebbings too,
>   Often above himself, sometimes below,
>   *Thou* always best."

9

In 1645 *Milton*, whose first published verses had been the Epitaph to the First Folio, mentions Shakespeare in "L'Allegro" as

> "Sweetest Shakspere, Fancy's child;"

and again mentions him in prose in 1649.

Samuel Sheppard, in 1646, writes of Shakespeare:—

> "Who wrote his lines with a sunbeam,
> More durable than time or fate."

William Bell, 1651, writes of Shakespeare's "alchemy."

Jasper Mayne, 1651, writing, I believe, of Beaumont and Fletcher, says:—

> "In thee Ben Jonson still held Shakspere's quill."

Sir William Dugdale, in 1653, mentions Shakespeare's monument made by Gerard Johnson.

Samuel Holland, in 1656, criticised his "Wit and Fancy in a Maze."

John Evelyn writes to Pepys, in 1689, describing a picture of Shakespeare at Lord Clarendon's in one piece with Chaucer and Beaumont and Fletcher.

In 1664 *Mary Cavendish, Duchess of Newcastle*, writes: "Shakspere had a clear judgment, a quick wit, a spreading fancy, a subtle observation, and a deep apprehension."

Dryden says, in 1668 : " To begin with Shakspere, he who of all the moderns had the largest and most comprehensive soul."

In the *Prologue* to " Julius Cæsar," printed 1672, we hear that

" In imitation Jonson's wit was shown,
 Heaven made *his* men, Shakspere made his own ! "

Dryden makes several mentions of him between 1672 and 1690, as follows : " Shakspere, who many times has written better than any Poet in any language." " In my style I propose to imitate the Divine Shakspere." " To return once more to Shakspere, no man ever drew so many characters."

In the *Preface* to " Troilus and Cressida," 1679, we have : —

" See, my loved Britons, see your Shakspere rise,
 An awful ghost confessed to human eyes."

Abraham Cowley, in his " Counterfeit Pieces," in 1680, says : —

" Our Shakspere wrote too in an age as blest,
 The happiest Poet of his time and best."

Georges de Scudéri says, in 1681 : " None ever exceeded him."

In 1682 *John Banks,* in the dedication of " Anna Bullen," wrote : " I say not this to derogate from those excellent persons, but to persuade them as Homer and our Shakspere did to immortalise the places where they were born."

Knightly Chetwood, in 1684, wrote: " Shakspere said all that Nature could impart."

In the manuscript biographical notices of Fulman and Davies, in 1690, remarks concerning Shakespeare appear.

Before the close of the seventeenth century, Dr. Ingleby finds *thirteen additional allusions* to the Plays. I have used some of his references in the biographical sketch in this volume to illustrate special points.

From a manuscript book belonging to *Sir Alexander Bowell* at the time of the Restoration, Dr. Ingleby quotes " Shakspere upon the King" as follows :—

" Crownes have their compass, length of days their date,
  Triumphs their tombs, felicity her fate,
  Of more than Earth, cann Earthe make none partaker,
  But knowledge makes the King most like his Maker," —

words that are worth preserving on the mere chance of their being his.

Mr. Halliwell-Phillipps thinks Dr. Ingleby ought to add to the " Centurie of Prayse" the following verses, written by *Samuel Sheppard*, about the

year 1635, only nineteen years after the poet's
death : —

> " Shakspere the next, who wrote so much, so well,
> That, when I view his bulke, I stand amazed ;
> A genius so inexhaustible
> That hath such tall and numerous trophies raised.
> Let him bee thought a block, an infidell,
> Shall dare to skreene the lustre of his praise ;
> Whose works shall find their due, a deathlesse date,
> Scorning the teeth of time or force of Fate ! "

DIRECT ASCRIPTION OF AUTHORSHIP TO SHAKESPEARE.

FROM VARIOUS SOURCES.

DIRECT ASCRIPTION OF AUTHORSHIP TO SHAKESPEARE.

" THE Witt's Recreation," published in 1640, says: " Let thine own histories prove thy Chronicle."

Richard Browne had said the same in 1638.

John Benson, in 1640, publishes Shakespeare's " Excellent and Sweetly Composed Poems."

John Warren does the same in the same year.

In 1598 *Gabriel Harvey* writes : " The younger sort take much delight in Shakspere's ' Venus and Adonis ;' but his ' Lucrece,' and ' Hamlet, Prince of Denmark ' have it in them to please the wiser sort."

Spenser, author of " The Faerie Queene," writes in 1594 : —

" Whose muse, full of high thought's invention,
    Doth like himself heroically sound."

Thomas Prujean, in 1644, names Shakespeare's Plays by title.

James Howell, in 1647, criticises Shakespeare in his plays as having " grown madde to make the muse welter in blood."

Twenty-one notices of the performance of Shake-speare's Plays are given by *Samuel Pepys* in the years 1659 and 1660.

In a Prologue to *Davenant's* " Enchanted Island," in 1669, it is said : —

> " So from old Shakspere's honored dust this day,
> Springs up and buds a new reviving play.
> But Shakspere's magic could not copied be;
> Within that circle none doth walk but he."

In 1669 *Edward Phillips* calls " Shakspere first of dramatic writers."

In 1677 *Sir Carr Scrope* says: " Never any rep-resented nature more to the life; his birth is the greatest honor Stratford can boast."

In the Dedicatory Epistle of *Thomas Shadwell* to an edition of 1678, he says : " I am now to pre-sent your Grace with the ' History of Timon;' and it is the more worthy of you, since it has the inimitable hand of Shakspere in it."

Thomas Rymer, in 1678, and *Martyn Herring-man* and *Mariot* propose to reprint the Plays in 1679.

In 1680 *Sir William Temple* speaks of Shake-speare " as the first to open the comic vein."

Sir George Raynsford, in 1682, says in a Pro-logue : —

"Yet we presume we may be safe to-day,
Since Shakspere gave foundation to the play."

John Sheffield, Earl Mulgrave, wrote in 1682 : —

"Shakspere and Fletcher are the wonders now.
Consider them and read them o'er and o'er.
Go see them played ; then read them as before."

J. Crown, in Prologue to "King Henry VI.,"
1681, writes : —

"To-day we bring old gathered Herbs, 't is true,
But such as in sweet Shakspere's Garden grew,
And all *his* plants immortal you esteem."

In 1689 *Nahum Tate*, in the Dedication to
"King Lear," says : —

"He hopes since in rich Shakspere's soil it grew
'T will relish yet with those whose tastes are true."

A copy of "King Lear" published in 1605, has
written upon it,

"First written by Mr. William Shakspere."

There are *seventeen contemporary notices* which
include his name in print.

Francis Meres, in 1598, quoted at length elsewhere, calls him "excellent for the stage in both
tragedy and comedy."

"Friendly Shakspere's tragedies" are spoken
of in "Diaphantes," 1604.

John Davies addresses him thus in his " Scourge of Follie," 1610 : —

" To our English Terence, Mr. Will Shakspere :
 " Some say, good Will, which I in sport do sing,
  Hadst thou not played some kingly parts in sport,
  Thou hadst been a companion for a king
  And been a king among the meaner sort.
  Some others raile ; but raile as they think fit
  Thou hast no railing but a raigning wit ;
  And honesty thou sowest which they do reape
  So to increase the stocke which they do keep."

The conclusion of the dedication of *Webster's* " White Devil," 1612, speaks of " the right happy and copious industry of Shakspere " in the same line as that of Beaumont and Fletcher.

In the Second Folio, 1632, *Hugh Holland* says :

 " His dayes are done that made the dainty playes
  Which crowned him Poet first, then Poets' king."

In 1614 *Thomas Freeman* wrote : —

 " Besides in plaies thy wit flows like Meander."

That *nineteen spurious plays* were attributed to Shakespeare is a very significant fact. It shows us unequivocally the value of his supposed authorship to the publisher, and implies an immense popularity. Of what other author was the same thing true ?

It is also certain that Shakespeare frequently altered old plays for the use of the theatres with which he was connected. In many instances the traces of his hand are clear. Can any one imagine that Lord Bacon ever had the power or the good will to undertake such a task?

HALLIWELL–PHILLIPPS.

HALLIWELL–PHILLIPPS.

MR. J. O. HALLIWELL–PHILLIPPS, to whose labours all English-speaking people are so greatly indebted, is a gentleman of wealth residing at Hollingbury Copse, Brighton, England. His "Outlines of the Life of Shakespeare" is only one of his many contributions to Shakespearean study. It has passed through five editions, in an enormous double octavo, between 1872 and 1885. I have been able to obtain only the first, third, and fifth editions; and so clumsily are these valuable books made up, that the comparison of the different editions is made with great difficulty. There is what seems like a capricious change of arrangement as the different editions succeed each other. There is no complete index to either, no table of contents, no list of illustrations. In the fifth edition, ten plans and prints have no label whatever, nor is there any way in which a novice could discover their relation to the text. The best way to alter a book like this would be to retain the original form and add the necessary annotations. New documents should be printed as supplements; but, above all, each new edition should be furnished with a preface, showing what is omitted, what is added, and what new points are made. In the third edition of the "Outlines," about three hundred illustrative notes are added, which refer to the main text by page and line. The text itself does not refer to the notes.

In the fifth edition all this is changed. The notes are numbered, the references to page and line are dropped. Numbers on the margin of the text refer to the notes; but there is no way of referring back to the text from the notes, unless one makes the references for himself with pen and ink, as I have done.

Greater inconvenience could hardly be. It seems ungracious to find fault with what is so generously given; but I should be sorry to see some literary hack reconstruct this noble work; and I have been indebted to Mr. Halliwell-Phillipps for so much, that I would willingly make it more.

In the first edition of his "Outlines of the Life of Shakespeare," Mr. Halliwell-Phillipps does not seem to have classified his various documents as carefully as in later editions.

In the third edition, published in 1883, we find:

Contemporary Notices	18
Theatrical Evidences	20
Registers of Copyright	34
Lifetime Editions	71
In all	143

mentions of the poet.

Also, Domestic Records	14
Biographical Notices	6
Records of Real Estate	38
In all	58

In judging of the position of Shakespeare before the public of his own century, by the number of published notes of himself or his performances, we must not forget that in his time there were no newspapers and no magazines. The first newspaper was published in England in 1622, — six years after the poet's death, — and no such thing as a magazine or periodical existed until long after. It is doubtful whether any well-known modern author could show a better record when this exception is made.

CONTEMPORARY EVIDENCES.

[*Abstracts from Halliwell-Phillipps.*]

FROM *Payne Collier :* —

When the Corporation of London threatened to interfere with the players at Blackfriars', the Earl of Southampton addressed a letter to the Lord Chancellor Ellsmere, introducing Shakespeare and Burbage.   After commenting on the talent and industry of Burbage, Southampton speaks of Shakespeare as no less deserving favour, and his "owne especial friende," the writer of some of the best English plays, and a favourite of both Elizabeth and James.

"This other hath to name William Shakspere," he says; "and they are both of one countie, and, indeed, almost of one town. Both are right famous in their qualities, though it belongeth not to your Lordship's gravity and wisdom to resort unto the places where they are wont to delight the public ear. Their trust and suit now is, not to be molested in their way of life, whereby they maintain themselves and their wives and families, — being both married and of good reputation, — as well as the widows and orphans of some of their dead fellowes."

This letter has been decided by Dr. C. M. Ingleby to be a forgery. As late as 1872 it was quoted by Halliwell-Phillipps, but it is not to be found in the third edition of his "Outlines" printed ten years later.

From "Poems in Divers Humors," printed in 1598, and again in 1605, Mr. Halliwell-Phillipps quotes mention of Spenser, Drayton, and Daniel,

> "And Shakspere, thou whose honey-flowing vaine,
> Pleasing the world thy praises doth obtaine,
> Live ever you, at least in fame, live ever!"

In "A Comparative Discourse on English Poets," by *Francis Meres*, published 1598, we have: —

"As the Greek tongue is made famous by Euripides, Aristophanes, *et al.*, so is the English by Spenser, Shakspere, and Marlowe. The sweet soul of Ovid lives in the mellifluous and honie-tongued Shakspere. As Plautus and Seneca are accounted best in tragedy and comedy among the Latins, so is Shakspere among the English, — most excellent in both kinds for the stage. If the Muses would speak English, they would speak with Shakspere's fine filèd phrase."

In "An Epigram on Shakspere," printed by *John Weemer* in 1599, he says: —

> "Honie-tongued Shakspere, when I saw thine issue,
> I swore Apollo got them, and no other."

In the "Garden of the Muses," printed in 1600, Shakespeare is quoted as the peer of Daniel, Spenser, Ben Jonson, and Marlowe. This was in his lifetime.

In "Diaphantes," published in 1604, poets are adjured to appeal to common sympathies, —

> "To come home to the vulgar element,
>   Like friendly Shakspere's tragedies."

In this respect, Shakespeare was a great contrast to Bacon, who hired Ben Jonson to translate his works into Latin, because he considered *that* the language of scholars, and did not believe in the immortality of the English tongue.

In *Camden's* "Remains," printed in 1605, Shakespeare is mentioned as "one of the most pregnant wits of our time."

In the "Return from Parnassus," 1606, we are told, —

> "His sweeter verse contains hart-robbing life."

In "Polimantheia," or "Means Lawful or Unlawful to Judge of a Commonwealth," printed at Cambridge in 1595, there are two marginal references to Shakespeare, as if to support positions taken.

In "A Comparative Discourse on English Poets,"

printed by *Francis Meres* in 1598, Shakespeare is used as an illustration four times.

Ben Jonson writes at length of him in his "Discoveries" in 1641, but I have used the quotation elsewhere.

John Davis mentions him as follows in the "Scourge of Follie," printed in 1610 : —

> "To our English Terence, Will Shakspere."

In the "Excellence of the English Tongue," printed in 1614, *Richard Carew* says : "Will you read Virgil ? Take the Earle of Surrey. Catullus ? Shakspere and Barlowe's Fragment."

In an *Epigram* by *Thomas Freeman*, 1614, he says : —

> "But to praise thee right, I want thy store,
> Then let thine own workes thine own worth appraise,
> And help adorn thee with deservèd bayes."

In the "General Chronicle of England," 1614, Shakespeare is named as the equal of Drayton, Marlowe, Ben Jonson, and others, "worthily flourishing by his own worke."

TWENTY THEATRICAL EVIDENCES

are cited by Halliwell-Phillipps. Among t
is found a *Poem* by *Leonard Digges*, prefixed
Thomas Cotes's edition of the Poems of Willia
Shakspere, Gent., London, 1640, from which
take the following : —

> "Poets are born, not made; when I would prove
> The truth, the glad remembrance I must love
> Of never-dying Shakspere, who alone
> Is argument enough to make that one.
> First, that he *was* a Poet none would doubt
> That heard the applause of what he sees set out,
> Imprinted ; — when thou hast, I will not say
> Reader, his *Workes*, for to contrive a play
> To him, 't was none, the pattern of all wit.
> Art without art unparalleled as yet.
> Next, Nature only helpt him, for look thorow
> This whole booke, thou shalt find he doth not borrow
> One phrase from Greeks, nor Latines imitate,
> Nor once from vulgar languages translate,
> Nor, plagiar-like, from others gleane,
> Nor begs he from each witty friend a scene
> To piece his Acts with ; all that he doth write
> Is pure his owne, — Plot, language exquisite.
> But oh ! what praise more powerful can we give
> The dead, than that by him the king's men live ?
>   . . . .
> Like old coined gold, his lines in every page
> Shall pass true current to succeeding age.
> But why do I dead Shakspere's praise recite ?
> Some second Shakspere must of Shakspere write."

This is valuable, not as fine poetry, but as a contemporaneous testimony to Shakespeare's ability. There is no question that the author recognizes the poetical gift, the power of rapid writing and of dramatic characterization, as well-known gifts of Shakespeare, which no one then living would dispute.

There are *thirty-three copyright entries* of Shakespeare's Plays between 1593 and 1623; that is more than one every year.

There are *seventy-one editions* of plays or poems, to which his name was attached, printed in his lifetime.

Upon the titlepage of *sixteen* of these are the words " *newly corrected* " or " *augmented* by William Shakspere."

From the pages of the First Folio, printed in 1623, we can extract varied testimonials.

Heminges and Condell, friends of Shakespeare, to whom he had left money in his will to buy funeral rings, dedicated it to his friends Pembroke and Montgomery. It is printed, they say, " to keep the memory of so worthy a friend and fellow."

They go on to say : " We most humbly consecrate to your Highnesses these remaines of your servant Shakspere, that the delight in them may be ever your Lordships', the reputation his, and the faults, if any, ours."

After expressing their regret that he did not live to print his own works, they go on : —

"Who, as he was a Happie imitator of Nature, was a most gentle expresser of it. His mind and hand went together ; and what he thought he uttered with that easiness that we have scarce received from him a blot in his papers."

On the same pages we find this noble tribute from *Ben Jonson* : —

> " My Shakspere, rise, I will not lodge thee by
> Chaucer or Spenser, or bid Beaumont lie
> A little further, to make thee a roome.
> Thou art a moniment without a tombe,
> And art alive still, while thy booke doth live,
> And we have wits to read and praise to give. . . .
> Triumph, my Britain, thou hast one to show,
> To whom all scenes of Europe homage owe ;
> He was not for an age, but for all time. . . .
> Nature herself was proud of his designs,
> And joyed to wear the dressing of his lines ;
> Yet must I not give Nature all.   Thy art,
> My gentle Shakspere, must enjoy a part,
> For though the Poet's matter Nature be,
> His art doth give the fashion. . . .
>   Look how the father's face
> Lives in his issue."

In these last words *Jonson* tells us what I think we all feel, that Shakespeare's character is shown in the lofty tendencies of his verse. If a man who knew Shakespeare intimately could write these lines concerning him when he was really, as we have heard him called, a low-born drunkard, absolutely incapable of the great works which go by his name, then we must make an end of all faith in man's written word.

Further on *Leonard Digges* says : —

> "This booke
> When brasse and marble fade, shall make thee looke
> Fresh to all ages."

J. M. says, in allusion to the habits of the stage :

> "We thought thee dead, but this, thy printed worth
> Tells thy Spectators that thou wentst but forth
> To enter with applause."

To all this we may add, in conclusion, *John Milton's* beautiful lines, the first verses ever printed by him. He was twenty-four years old when the Second Folio was printed. He was only seven when Shakespeare died; but testimony coming so close, from so great a man distinguished for the austerity of his own life, is quite as good as if it were contemporaneous : —

> "What needs my Shakspere for his honored bones
> The labor of an age in pilèd stones?
> Or that his hallowed relics should be hid,
> Under a star-y-pointing pyramid?

Dear son of memory, great heir of fame,
What need'st thou such weak witness of thy name ?
Thou in our wonder and astonishment
Hast built thyself a live-long monument.
For, whilst to the shame of slow endeavoring art,
Thy easy numbers flow, and that each heart
Hath from the leaves of thy unvalued book
Those Delphic lines with deep impression took,
Then, thou our Fancy of itself bereaving,
Dost make us marble with too much conceiving
And so, sepulchred in such pomp dost lie,
That kings for such a tomb would wish to die."

It remains only to quote the verses of an unknown author upon the Stratford monument, and
three lines from the stone which covers the grave
of Shakespeare's oldest daughter, Susannah Hall.
On Shakespeare's monument are these words : —

" Read, if thou canst, whom envious Death hath placed
Within this monument : Shakespeare, with whom
Quick nature died, whose name doth deck this Tombe
Far more than cost ; sith all that he hath writ
Leaves living Art but page to serve his wit."

Of Susannah it is said : —

" Witty above her sex, but that's not all,
Wise to salvation was good mistress Hall.
Something of Shakspere was in that."

In 1600 a play called " The First Part of the
Life of Sir John Oldcastle," with which Shakespeare had nothing to do, and which did not even

belong to his own theatre, was published under his name, by one Thomas Pavior.

In 1608 Thomas Pavior again published a play with Shakespeare's name attached to it. It was called "The Yorkshire Tragedy," and as Shakespeare was then travelling on the southern coast, he may never have heard of it.

The use of Shakespeare's name to give currency to poor plays, shows that he was a well-known author, from whom good work was expected. On one or two occasions he interfered to prevent an unfair use of his name or his initials; and that he did not do it always, was probably due to his very busy life, his frequent absences on professional tours, or his sequestration at Stratford. There is no stronger testimony to the position he held in the public regard than the constant effort of publishers so long as he lived to attribute to him plays with which he had nothing to do. When the First Folio was printed, one half of its contents were new to the reading public, and it was evident that Shakespeare's friends knew what he had written and did not proceed on guess-work. They printed "Titus Andronicus" and the Third Part of "King Henry VI.," which no lover of Shakespeare would have been sorry to relinquish; but they omitted "The London Prodigal" and "The

Yorkshire Tragedy," which had been publicly ascribed to him.

Among the arguments used to fasten the authorship of Shakespeare's Plays upon Bacon is the use by the poet of localities which must have been familiar to Bacon by his descent or residence.

In the "Taming of the Shrew," played and printed before 1594, the Induction brings us into a hamlet of Stratford, and portrays by the names of Sly, Naps, Turf, and Pimpernell, persons well known and living there in Shakespeare's day. Wincot was a hamlet where Shakespeare had property and which he frequented; Sly was a servant of William Combe, of whom Shakespeare once bought a hundred acres of land. There is a tradition that Shakespeare frequented the ale-houses of that hamlet to make himself familiar with the ways of a fool there.

Now for many historical or national reasons, it was quite possible for Shakespeare to be well informed in regard to places and persons associated with Bacon. Every London man heard legends connected with Chiselhurst or St. Albans, while it was not in the least likely that Bacon ever heard of Wincot fools, or had sufficient sympathy with the comic side of humble life to make acquaintance with the servants of William Combe.

Mr. Halliwell-Phillipps gives us many small points tending to identify the writer of the Plays with a resident of Stratford and its neighbourhood. One of these is the use of the phrase " Aroint thee," to be found only in the Plays of Shakespeare and the legal records of Stratford.   When Ulysses tells his "love-embarrassed colleague" that,

" The fool slides o'er the ice that you should break ; "

he expresses a daily human experience in so uncommon a way, that we know some actual occurrence must have suggested the form.   Mr. Halliwell-Phillipps discovers this in a local adventure of a certain Jack Miller, a petted innocent of Esom, who crossed the Avon in infatuated pursuit of a professional buffoon, where the ice was so weak that it sank at every step, and went to pieces under a brickbat thrown by a spectator who was afterwards one of Shakespeare's theatrical colleagues.   The story was in print in 1600.

NOTE.

IN March, 1599, Essex went to Ireland, and Southampton was his General of Horse. In May or June, Shakespeare, the "especial friend" of Southampton, inserted a graceful compliment to him in his Play of "King Henry V.," which indicates his sympathy with the love and expectation of the people.

On Feb. 2, 1603, Shakespeare was summoned to Whitehall to act before Elizabeth for the last time. On the 24th of March the Queen died. In spite of many marks of her favour he wrote no verse of eulogy or lamentation. His silence was remarked, for more than one of the smaller poets called upon him by name to bewail the dead Queen. He never forgave the Queen who put Essex to death, and we may judge therefore that he was as little likely to serve the purposes of Bacon, who betrayed him, and needlessly prosecuted the charges of the Government against him.

"A Mournful Dittie" entitled "Elisabeth's Losse" has the following verse : —

> "You poets all, brave Shakspere, Johnson, Greene,
> Bestow your time to write for England's Queene ;
> Re-turn your Songs, your Sonnets, and your Layes
> To set forth sweet Elisabeth (a's) praise."

The author of "Epigrams," published in 1604, in speaking of the death of Elizabeth, says some dare to praise her, —

> " Some other humbly craves
> For help of spirits in their sleeping graves,
> As he that called to Shakspere, Jonson, Greene,
> To write of their dead noble Queene."

In 1603 Henry Chettle wrote : —

> "Nor doth the silver tonguèd Melicent
> Drop from his honied muse one sable teare
> To mourn her death that gracèd his desert,
> And to his layes opened her royal eare ;
> Shepherd, remember our Elisabeth,
> And sing her Rape done by that Tarquin Death."

Another verse of the " Mournful Dittie " says :

> " You Poets all, brave Shakspere, Johnson, Greene,
> Bestow your time to write for England's Queen ;
> Lament, lament, lament, you English peers,
> Lament your losse, possessed so many years."

Many things united to destroy the respect of such a man as Shakespeare for the Queen. Southampton had married without her consent, and she never forgave him, and summarily dismissed him from the post to which Essex had appointed him. "As You Like It" was performed by Shakespeare's company during Essex's imprisonment, and any attentive reader of it will think that it might

11

have been written for the especial comfort of
Southampton in 1601. The compliment to Elizabeth, so often quoted from "King Henry VIII.,"
was not personal to the author. It is put into
the lips of Cranmer. If this be no explanation,
we can say farther that between the death of
Essex and the appearance of this Play there was
time for much softening of the resentment which
his execution occasioned.

DOMESTIC RECORDS.

1. THE *will* of *Robert Arden,* dated November, 1556, which gives the poet's mother, Mary Arden, the farm of Asbyes in Wincote, the "crop in the ground," and some money before the estate was divided. It makes her and her sister Alis executors, and leaves some money to the town.

2. The *inventory* of *Robert Arden's* estate. This included certain articles of luxury, such as tapestries or "peynted clothes." It is not a complete inventory of household effects. His bedsteads and some other things seem to have belonged to his second wife, Agnes.

3. The *will* of *Agnes Arden,* Shakespeare's step-grandame on his mother's side.

4. The *inventory* of *Agnes Arden's* estate, which contains tapestries and the missing bedsteads.

5. The *will* of a certain *Richard Hathaway* of Shottery, made in 1581. It mentions children, — Thomas, John, William, Agnes, Catharine, and Margarett, but *not Anne.* This man is the Hathaway usually supposed to be the father of Shakespeare's wife, but this is impossible. He was dead in July, 1582, and Shakespeare did not marry Anne until the following November. The seal of

Richard Hathaway said to be attached to Shakespeare's marriage license must have belonged to some other person, of whom Anne may have been daughter or ward.

6. *Bond against impediments*. Given in anticipation of the marriage of Shakespeare and Anne Hathaway, Nov. 28, 1582. This made any other marriage illegal. This was discovered among the papers at the Consistorial Court of Worcester, a county which touched Warwickshire. Bonds were given by two persons said to be friends and neighbours of the Hathaways, to indemnify the Bishop of Worcester for licensing the marriage with only one publishment of the banns. This is sometimes, but I believe improperly, called Shakespeare's marriage license, and the seal of one Richard Hathaway is said to be attached to it. Whatever were the causes that prevented an earlier marriage between William and Anne, it seems impossible that they should have been considered discreditable. Shakespeare's great success made him a fair target for the shafts of envy. In London, in his dramatic career, he was associated with men who came from his own neighbourhood, who must have known every detail of his history, who never attained a celebrity to compare with that of the " Shake-Scene " whom they scoffed at. If there

had been any scandal connected with Shakespeare's marriage it would have been sure to come to publicity in his lifetime.

7. A *draft* of a grant *of coat armour*, for which Shakespeare's father petitioned in 1569, and which had been granted. This recounts the services of a grandfather rewarded by Henry VII. for services on the field, and rights obtained by marriage with Mary Arden. The arms applied for were certainly carried by Shakespeare and his descendants; but the value of this paper consists in the fact that no man as obscure and poverty-stricken as John Shakespeare is frequently represented would have dared to make such an application. It would have been against all the proprieties of the period.

8. A *letter* from *Abraham Sturley* to Richard Quiney, Jan. 24, 1597–98, in which reference is made to an intended purchase by the poet at Shottery, and Quiney is advised to suggest to him an investment in Stratford tithes.

This investment in tithes requires a certain amount of explanation; all the more, that it seems to have added greatly to Shakespeare's wealth. Previous to the Reformation and for some time after, the clergy, being frightened about the security of their properties, took in many cases bonuses for long leases. In this way the Stratford tithes had been leased out, and Shakespeare finally bought the remaining term of one half.

9. A *return* of the quantity of *corn and malt* held in February, 1598, by the inhabitants of the quarter in which " New Place " was situated, " William Shakspere ten quarters." This was, with one exception, the largest quantity credited to any one man in the town.

10. A *letter* from *Adrian Quiney* to his son Richard (1599 ?). He " may bargain with William Shakspere," probably about the town tithes.

11. A *letter* from *Abraham Sturley* to Richard Quiney, Nov. 4, 1598, speaks of Shakespeare as likely to procure money for the Corporation, and to receive a lease of the tithes if he chooses and can raise thirty or forty pounds.

12. A *draft* of a grant of *coat armour* proposed to be conferred on John Shakespeare, 1599. Original from the college-at-arms. Duplicate of paper of 1596.

13. A *declaration* filed by *William Shakspere* in the Court of Record of Stratford on Avon, in the year 1604, to recover the value of malt sold to one *Philip Rogers*.

14. Precepts in an *action for debt* brought by *Shakespeare* against *John Addenbroke*, in the Stratford-upon-Avon Court of Record, 1609.

BIOGRAPHICAL NOTICES.

1. FROM *Ben Jonson's* "Timber," or "Discoveries made upon Men and Matter as they have
flowed out of his Daily Reading," etc., fol., London,
1641 : —

"I remember the players have often mentioned
it as an honor to Shakspere, that in his writing,
whatsoever he penned, he never blotted a line.
My answer hath beene : 'Would he had blotted
a thousand !' which they thought a malevolent
speech. I had not told posterity this, but for the
ignorance of those who choose that circumstance
to commend their friend by, wherein hee most
faulted, and to justifie mine own Candour ; for I
loved the man, and doe honour his memorie on
this side idolatrie as much as any.

"Hee was indeed honest, and of an open and
free nature ; had an excellent phantasie, brave
notions, and gentle expressions, wherein hee flowed
with that facilitie that sometime it was necessary
hee should be stopped. His wit was in his own
power ; would the rule of it had been so too.

"Many times hee fell into those things could
not escape laughter, as when hee said of Cesar,
one speaking to him : 'Cesar, thou dost me

wrong;' hee replied, 'Cesar did never wrong but with just cause,' and such like, which were ridiculous. But he redeemed his vices with his virtues. There was ever more in him to be praysed than to be pardoned."

2. From *Fuller's* "Worthies," 1662 : —

"Plautus was never any scholar, as doubtless our Shakspere, if alive, would confess himself."

3. From the notes of *Rev. John Ward,* vicar of Stratford in 1662. He says : —

"Shakspere was a natural wit, without any art at all. In his later years he lived at Stratford, and supplied the stage with two playes every year. He spent at the rate of a thousand pounds a year."

4. From *Aubrey's* "Lives of Eminent Men," 1680 : —

"Shakspere was a handsome, well-shaped man, very good company, and of a very ready and pleasant wit. The humor of ——, the constable in the 'Midsummer Night's Dream,' he happened to take at Grendon in Bucks, and there was living that constable in 1642, when I first came to Oxford.

"Though Ben Jonson says of him that he had 'little Latine and lesse Greeke,' he understood Latin pretty well, for he had been a schoolmaster in the country in his youth."

There is no constable in the "Midsummer

Night's Dream;" and Elbow, the constable in
" Measure for Measure," is probably the character
intended.   It is strange that the very credible
statement that Shakespeare was a schoolmaster
in the country in his youth, made by Aubrey
on the authority of a " Mr. Beeston," has attracted so little attention.   It is to Aubrey that
we owe the scandal in reference to Sir William
Davenant, which has been abundantly disproved
by Mr. Halliwell-Phillipps. In spite of proof, the
scandal is continually repeated.   In his Plays
Shakespeare several times shows a keen sense of
the humorous side of a schoolmaster's position,
and this alone should have drawn some attention
to Mr. Beeston's assertion.

5. From a *manuscript account* of places in *Warwickshire,* written in 1693, by a person named
Dowdall : —

" He was the best of his family; but the male
line is extinguished.   Not one, for feare of the
curse above-said, dare touch his grave-stone, though
his wife and daughters did earnestly desire to be
laid in the same grave with him."

Fuller says of him that " he was jocular, and
inclining to festivity."

Rowe writes in his " Account of the Life of
Shakspere," 1709 : —

"His family were of good figure and fashion then, and they are mentioned as gentlemen. His father, though he was a considerable dealer in wool, had so large a family that, though he was his eldest son, he could give him no better education than his own employment. The poet was a good-natured man of great sweetness in his manners, and a most agreeable companion."

Dryden, 1672, preserves a remark of Shakespeare's to the effect that, in "Romeo and Juliet," he was "obliged to kill Mercutio in the third act, lest he should have been killed by him"!

It is painful to be obliged to give up *Spenser's* tribute to "pleasant Willy," in the "Tears of the Muses;" but Spenser died seventeen years before Shakespeare, and it is now generally conceded that those lines refer to one Richard Tarlton, a famous comedian of that time, who owed this sobriquet to some special part that he played. Tarlton died while Spenser was writing in 1588.

Webster, in the dedication to the "White Devil," 1612, speaks of "the right happy and copious industry of Shakspere," just four years before his death.

In spite of the Puritanical feeling in Stratford, which forbade theatrical performances by law in 1612, and which in 1622 gave the "king's play-

ers" "six shillings" for "*not* performing in the
town hall," some friend had the courage to in-
scribe on Shakespeare's monument, with the
probable consent of the Halls, words which bear
witness to the fact that his genius was abundantly
recognized in his own time : —

> "Shakespeare, with whom
> Quick nature died, whose name does deck this Tombe
> Far more than cost.'

Mary Harte, a descendant of Joan Shakespeare,
who lived till 1750, stated that the organization
of "Shakespeare's boys," who held horses at the
theatres, grew out of the accident of the poet's
performing this service for a gentleman on his
first arrival.

RECORDS CONCERNING ESTATES.

1. A CONVEYANCE by *Robert Arden,* Shakespeare's maternal grandfather, of a house and land at Snitterfield, in trust for his three daughters, July 17, 1550. This farm was then occupied by Richard Shakespeare, the poet's paternal grandfather.

2. *Concord* of a *fine levied* on the occasion of the *purchase by John Shakespeare* of two houses at Stratford on Avon, 1575.

3. *Note* of a *fine levied* when the estate of *Asbyes was mortgaged* by the Shakespeares at the Easter term, 1578.

4. *Deed of conveyance* on the 15th of October, 1579, from Shakespeare's parents to *Robert Webbe,* of their interest in property at Snitterfield. This is one of the papers in which John Shakespeare is distinctly characterized as a *yeoman.*

5. *Bill of complaint* brought by *John Shakespeare,* the poet's father, against *Lambert* in the Court of Queen's Bench, 1589, respecting an estate at Wilmecote, near Stratford. From the Coram Rege Rolls. *This document contains the only positive notice of the poet between the years 1585 and 1592.*

6. *Deed of conveyance* from *John Shakespeare* to *George Badger,* of a slip of land belonging to the

birthplace estate, 1596–97. In this instrument
John Shakespeare is called *yeoman*.

7. *Papers in a Chancery suit* respecting the estate of *Asbyes*, 1598.

The father and mother of William Shakespeare
were the plaintiffs, and Edmund Lambert, the
poet's uncle by marriage, the defendant.

The Shakespeares state that in consideration of
a loan of £40 they mortgaged the estate to Lambert; that when they went according to agreement
and punctually to repay the money, Lambert refused to take it unless all moneys due on other
accounts were also paid. The said Lambert died;
and his son entering into possession had divided
and sold the property, so that they did not know
against whom to bring suit.

John Lambert replies substantially that the
Shakespeares promised to lift the mortgage on the
feast day of St. Michael, 1580, and to forfeit the estate if this were not done. He charges that this
was not done, and that the motive of the suit was
to take advantage of the increased value of the
farm, to obtain larger compensation for it.

The Shakespeares respond again that their
money, promptly tendered on St. Michael's feast
day, 1580, was refused unless all other moneys
due to Lambert were paid.

It does not appear that the Shakespeares were ever able to resume possession.

8. *Indenture of the conveyance* of over a hundred acres of land from *William and John Combe* to Shakespeare, May, 1602.

9. Extract from the *Court Rolls of the Manor of Rowington*, being the surrender from *Walter Getly* to William Shakespeare of *premises in Chapel Lane*, Stratford on Avon, 1602.

10. *The conveyance* to William Shakespeare of the moiety of a *lease of the tithes* in and near Stratford upon Avon, July 24, 1605. From the town records.

11. *A conveyance of Premises* adjoining the birthplace in *Henley Street*, July 20, 1609.

12. *Note* of a *fine levied* in Trinity term, 1610, on the estate purchased by Shakespeare from the *Combes*.

13. *Draft* of a *bill of complaynt* respecting the *tithes*, Shakespeare being one of the plaintiffs, 1612. This assumes that Shakespeare and others have been obliged to pay taxes unpaid by certain " men of ability," in order to save their own estates and protect those of poorer men, and demands redress.

14. *A conveyance of Premises* adjoining the birthplace of the poet in *Henley Street*, in which Shakespeare is mentioned, Jan. 22, 1613.

15. *The deed* of *Bargain and Sale of the Black-friars' estate* to William Shakespeare and trustees, March 10, 1612–13.

This indenture was one handed over to the poet after it had been enrolled by the vendor in the Court of Chancery.

16. A *duplicate of the preceding,* — original in the Library of the City of London. This duplicate is signed by Shakespeare; No. 15, by Henry Walker, vendor. Mr. Halliwell-Phillipps expresses an odd sort of wonder that there should be *two* copies of this indenture; but surely in any transaction between *two* parties, each party is entitled to a copy of the paper which binds him, and in ordinary legal business to-day this right is claimed.

17. *Deed* from Shakespeare and trustees to Henry Walker, *mortgaging the Blackfriars' estate* to Walker, March 11, 1612. Signed.

18. *Articles of Agreement* between William Shakespeare and *William Replingham*, by which Replingham agrees to compensate the poet, should loss accrue to him from enclosures contemplated by Replingham, 1614.

NOTE.

12

NOTE.

THE confirmation of my theory that John Shakespeare retired from the town of Stratford soon after the mortgage of Asbyes in 1578, and occupied some other rural property in the hope of again possessing the Arden estate, can only be found in the history of the various farms inherited by the poet. No doubt Mr. Halliwell-Phillipps has searched the Warwickshire records over and over again, but *not with this end in view.* He has always been looking for details relating to John Shakespeare's greater son.

In Shakespeare's will and in three different legal instruments for the resettlement of his estate after his death, he is mentioned as having *inherited* property in Stratford upon Avon, Old Stratford, Bishopton, and Welcombe. These properties in Bishopton and Welcombe may have been a portion of land bestowed upon the late " ante-cessor" who had served Henry VII.

In 1578 the Asbyes property was mortgaged. In 1579 John Shakespeare and Mary Arden sold their Snitterfield "farms and messuages" to Robert Webbe. This was undoubtedly done to raise money for the redemption of Asbyes. When Edmund Lambert peremptorily refused to give up the estate until he received all other moneys due, the blow must have been a severe one. Edmund had married Joan Arden, who received only a small portion of the estates of her father in comparison with Mary Shakespeare. But, in spite of this, cordial relations seem to have been sustained. Mary's first child was named Joan; and when this little one died, another born in 1569 received the same name. A son who was born in the very year after the mortgage was named Edmund. The fact that "other sums" were due to Lambert indicates that he was in the habit of lending John Shakespeare money to complete his various investments. If John had the genial nature of his oldest son, he would probably have been slow to detect any systematic attempt to get possession of Asbyes. It must have been to gratify his wife that John Shakespeare desired to impale the "arms of Arden" with those granted him in 1569.

Perhaps Joan Lambert was ambitious also. At all events, when John Shakespeare entered upon a chancery suit, which lasted not only through Edmund Lambert's life, but into that of his son

John, and as late as 1598, he knew not only that he had lost his wife's paternal estate, but that he had involved himself in an endless family quarrel, and was deprived of his most influential friend in the county. It is no wonder that, wounded in feeling beside, he forgot all about his "coats of armour," until he was again able to sustain them properly.

He would naturally wish to atone to his wife for the loss of her property. He had lived in one of the Henley-Street houses, and used the other as a warehouse for the storing and sale of wool, — a "wool-shop," as Mr. Halliwell-Phillipps calls it. He was never poor enough to sell these houses, never alienated a foot of his land, so far as we know, till he sold two small portions of land to two of his neighbours for their convenience in 1596–97.

Soon after his troubles began, I think, he must have removed to some property outside the town limits, leaving his daughter Joan in the Henley-Street house, and having fitted up the rooms over the wool-shop for the use of Shakespeare and his wife and family.

Writing in 1709, Rowe says that "John Shakspere was a considerable dealer in wool, who could do no better by his oldest son than to bring him up to his own employment."

What more natural than that he should take
charge of the wool-shop, and then, in English
fashion, have his apartments over his place of
business? If so, the "doors of interior communication," which are described as still existing between the two Henley-Street houses, would have
had a very natural origin; and it would be easier
to understand why in all documents the poet is
always mentioned as "William Shakspere of Stratford." It is quite clear that he never relinquished
his residence.

It seems to me, however, that the legal paper
numbered 11, and dated July, 1609, in the fore-
going list, offers some support to my view. This
paper is a conveyance of property adjoining and
bounded by the "wool shop." It is No. XXX.
of Halliwell-Phillipps's Documentary Appendix.
In it appears the following descriptive sentence:
"betweene the tenement of Thomas Hornbie on
the easte parte, and the tenement 'late' of William
Shakspere on the weste parte."

Mr. Halliwell-Phillipps says that although the
insertion of the word "late" is doubtless a clerical
error, it is right to draw attention to the fact that
it is an "interpolation;" that is, it was inserted
by the clerk, after the document was completed,
above the line.

Now how is it possible that such an *insertion* should be an *oversight?* And if so, why should it be repeated rather than corrected in another conveyance of the same estate in 1613? It is a proper legal phrase to designate not ownership but *tenancy,* well recognized as such at least in this country; and if William Shakespeare were the last prominent townsman who had occupied the house for any number of years, it would be the natural expression for the clerk to employ.

When these words were written, in 1609 and again in 1613, Shakespeare was alive and living at New Place, which he had purchased twelve years before the first entry. I could point to more than one instance where the phrase " late of " refers to a tenancy, which had expired thirty years before the words were written.

As far as can be inferred from known facts, Anne Hathaway was an orphan, whose connection with Shottery has been assumed ; and in that case her proper home in her husband's enforced absence would have been in the premises where he had helped to carry on his father's business, and in the protecting neighbourhood of his family.

CONCLUSION.

THE NEW POINTS.

CONCLUSION.

THE NEW POINTS.

THERE are several instances of repetition in this volume, but they are intentional. In making a new impression it is well to repeat evidence at every point where it can be supposed to have a natural bearing, and I have not shrunk from doing so.

I believe I have made several new points, but I may be mistaken. I wish to recapitulate them here, not so much to assert any claim to them, as to relieve the authors quoted in my pages from such responsibility for them as the general statement may seem to impose :—

1. I have given the history of the "coat of armour" in such a way as to make the application for it throw light on John Shakespeare's personal circumstances and standing. I cannot help thinking that the persistence with which this application was pressed, after the mortgage of Asbyes made it impossible to take up the first patent,

indicates more connection between the application and John Shakespeare's circumstances than is at first apparent. He may have angered the county gentlemen by his first application; and a willingness to see him defeated may have induced men of "wealth and ability" to stand by Edmund Lambert in what now seems a most unjust use of power. The second grant was made in 1596, and directly after Shakespeare files a bill "for the recovery of Asbyes." In this bill, he asks the protection of the court, stating that as regards this suit he stands almost alone, while his nephew is supported by men of "wealth and ability." It is not strange if this went on, and the whole county took occasion to sneer at the "new coat," that the poet took his revenge when the "Merry Wives of Windsor" came out in the next year, 1598; nor that his father insisted on permission to impale the arms of Arden in 1599.

2. I suggest that John Shakespeare went into the country, or at least into a suburb of Stratford, leaving the poet's family in the Henley-Street house, perhaps to attend to his town business. I think I find confirmation of the suggestion in legal phrases used during Shakespeare's lifetime and after his death.

3. I draw attention to the fact that Anne

Hathaway could not have been the daughter of Richard Hathaway of Shottery.

4. I make some new suggestions as to the erection and inscribing of the Stratford monument.

If these four suggestions, and some others of minor import to be found in these pages, are deemed unworthy of serious consideration, I shall not be sorry that I brought them forward. No house was ever built without a scaffolding, which is easily torn away when the builder's work is complete. These suggestions are the timbers by the aid of which I would rear a living structure. If they do not serve, let them fall.

In issuing a second edition of this little book, I wish to add here a few remarks that I shall hope at a later time to incorporate into their proper places.

In connection with the opinion I have expressed that Ben Jonson probably wrote the inscription on the Stratford monument, I copy the following from the Rev. William Harness : —

"The first syllable in 'Socratem' is here made short, which cannot be allowed. Perhaps we should read Sophoclem."

To any one acquainted with the inaccuracies of English stone-cutters in the early part of the seventeenth century, this will seem a very natural

solution of the puzzle which attends any connection of the name of Socrates with that of
Shakespeare.

By this substitution we get a perfect in place
of an imperfect dactyl, and good sense in the place
of nonsense, and the lines read : —

"Judicio Pylium genio Sophoclem, arte Maronem
Terra tegit populus mœret Olympus habet."

Words Ben Jonson was very likely to write.

In one of the notes to Spedding's "Life and Letters of Lord Bacon" it is mentioned that Sir William
Cooke, of the family of Ann Cooke, mother of
Francis Bacon, married Joyce Lucy, the only surviv-
ing issue of Sir Thomas Lucy. He died in 1618.

I think this note worth preserving, because it
shows how many trivial circumstances unknown
to us might easily conspire to prevent any intimacy
between Bacon and Shakespeare. It also makes
it seem very unlikely that Bacon could have
written the introduction to the "Merrie Wives
of Windsor."

In conclusion, I desire gratefully to acknowl-
edge that but for the unparalleled labour of Mr.
Halliwell-Phillipps it would not have been possible for any scholar out of England to venture
any suggestion concerning these facts in the hope
that it might prove of value.

INDEX.

INDEX.

ABERDEEN, 54.
Addenbroke, John, 59, 166.
Arden, Agnes, second wife of Robert, her will and inventory of property, 163.
——, Alice, 14, 163.
——, Robert, his lease of land at Snitterfield to Richard Shakespeare, 13, 109, 172; his ancestry and social rank, 14 ; the terms of his will and disposition of his property, 14, 15, 163; his conveyance of property to his daughters, 172.
Asbyes, estate of, inherited by Mary Arden, 14, 163; its mortgage by John Shakespeare, and subsequent suit for its recovery, 21, 26, 111, 113, 173, 179, 181, 188; proposed settlement of the difficulty, with its conveyance to the Lamberts, 112.
Aston, 15.
" As You Like It," 162.
Atwoode, Thomas, his bequest to Richard Shakespeare, 109.
Aubrey, quoted as to Shakespeare and his knowledge of Latin, 27, 168; as connected with the Davenant scandal, 56, 169.
Ayer, playwriter at Nuremberg, his supposed acquaintance with Shakespeare, 40.

BACON, DELIA, her rare personal gifts, 103, 104; her historical studies and lectures, 103, 104; her preliminary investigation and question of Shakespeare's authorship, 104; publishes her "Philosophy of Shakespeare's Plays," 105; Emerson's estimate of her ability, 106.
Bacon, Francis, 30, 79, 80, 150; his probable acquaintance with Shakespeare, 82, 83; his supposed authorship of the Plays considered, 158.
Badger, George, 172.
Bancroft, Thomas, his reference to Shakespeare, 128.
Banks, John, his mention of Shakespeare, 131.
"Banquet of Jests," its mention of Shakespeare and Stratford, 128.
Barnard, Sir John, his marriage with Elizabeth Hall, 74, 93.
Barnefield, Richard, 51; his mention of Shakespeare, 126.
Basse, William, his tribute to Shakespeare, 127.
Beaumont, 129, 130, 140.
Beecher, Catherine, 103.
Beeston, Mr., 27, 169.
Bell, Dr., his assumption of Shakespeare's visit to the Continent, 40.

University Press: John Wilson and Son, Cambridge.

#289 7230